D-Day 1944 (3)

Sword Beach & the British Airborne landings

Campaign • 105

D-Day 1944 (3)

Sword Beach & the British Airborne landings

Ken Ford · Illustrated by Howard Gerrard

Series editor Lee Johnson · *Consultant editor* David G Chandler

First published in Great Britain in 2002 by Osprey Publishing,
PO Box 883, Oxford, OX1 9PL, UK
PO Box 3985, New York, NY 10185-3985, USA
Email: info@ospreypublishing.com

Osprey Publishing is part of the Osprey Group.

Transferred to digital print on demand 2014.

First published 2002
12th impression 2012

Printed and bound in Great Britain

A CIP catalogue record for this book is available from the British Library.

ISBN: 978 1 84176 366 8

Series Editor: Lee Johnson
Design by The Black Spot
Index by Alan Thatcher
Maps by The Map Studio
3D bird's-eye views by The Black Spot
Battlescene artwork by Howard Gerrard
Originated by PPS Grasmere Ltd, Leeds, UK
Typeset in Helvetica Neue and ITC New Baskerville

Artist's note
Readers may care to note that the original paintings from which the colour plates
in this book were prepared are available for private sale. All reproduction copyright
whatsoever is retained by the Publisher. Enquiries should be addressed to:

Howard Gerrard
11 Oaks Road
Tenterden
Kent
TN30 6RD
UK

The Publishers regret that they can enter into no correspondence upon this matter.

The Woodland Trust
Osprey Publishing is supporting the Woodland Trust, the UK's leading woodland
conservation charity, by funding the dedication of trees.

www.ospreypublishing.com

Key to military series symbols

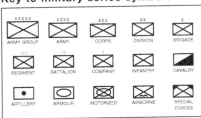

CONTENTS

ORIGINS OF THE BATTLE

The landings on Sword Beach and the battles fought by British paratroopers in the area around the estuary of the River Orne were just a small part of the great Allied liberation of Normandy that began on 6 June 1944. What happened in this left-hand sector of the invasion front was matched with equal ferocity by the fighting on four other beaches and on other landing places along a 50-mile stretch of coastline to the west. This book will try to explain why Sword Beach and the British airborne assault were so important to the overall success of the D-Day landings.

When the USA entered the war in December 1941 it declared war on all the Axis powers, but agreed with Britain that the European theatre would take priority over matters in the Far East. This 'Germany first' strategy pleased America's Russian and British allies, as it meant that all three nations could concentrate the bulk of their forces simultaneously against Hitler. A cross-Channel invasion by British and American forces then became inevitable, since it would provide the shortest and most effective route into Germany's heartland. Whilst this decision was the most sensible and desirable, Britain claimed that it would be impossible to mount such an amphibious attack until many seemingly insurmountable problems had been solved.

THE LESSONS OF DIEPPE

The most serious problem was the lack of sufficient shipping to carry the assaulting forces, more especially the dearth of landing-craft. Shipyards in Britain and America worked to full capacity to produce them, but even by the date of the planned invasion, totals still fell well short of demand. There was also no suitable plan for the invasion available, nor a proven set of tactics by which to launch the assault. Even four years into the war, in 1943, amphibious warfare was still very much in its infancy. There had been a few combined-operations raids on enemy shores, but none on a scale that provided pointers for the size of the invasion that was envisaged. A raid in force on the French coastal town of Dieppe in August 1942 did, however, provide valuable information regarding the problems of attacking an enemy-held port. The attempted landings were not a success. The troops that arrived on the main beach were pinned down on the shoreline and the tanks that were landed to support them could not cross the sea wall and floundered on the loose shingle. On either flank the story was basically the same; beach defences kept the troops confined to the water's edge and enemy machine-gun fire decimated them as they lay trapped in the open.

LEFT The build up of troops and equipment for D-Day was a massive undertaking. Every available space in southern England was put to good use to store stockpiles of vehicles and equipment ready for the invasion. This picture taken on 5 May 1944 shows unmarked Churchill and Cromwell tanks lined up along the Winchester by-pass, 15 miles from Southampton Docks, in preparation for their move to France. (Imperial War Museum, H38510)

7

The lessons of Dieppe were put to good use during the planning for Operation Overlord. The key factors were as follows: firstly, the assault would have to be made over open beaches and not against a fortified port area; secondly, support from naval guns and aircraft was essential to eliminate all enemy strongpoints; and thirdly, specialised weapons and armour designed for beach operations would have to be developed, to allow tanks and infantry to get off the beach and move inland. It was clear that the invasion would have to be a massive combined operation, rather than a series of battles fought by the three different services.

In May 1943, COSSAC (Chief of Staff to the Supreme Allied Commander) headed by Lieutenant-General Frederick Morgan, was set up to plan the cross-Channel invasion, taking into account all of the problems that had been raised and the solutions that had been offered to overcome them. Morgan and his team's task was to begin the critical initial planning for the invasion until the appointment of a Supreme Commander for the campaign.

In studying the possible sites for the assault, it soon became clear to COSSAC that the area of Normandy in the Bay of the Seine, between the estuary of the River Orne and the base of the Cotentin Peninsula, would be the most suitable location for the amphibious forces to come ashore. In arriving at this decision, LtGen Morgan had to take into account many factors; most significantly, he had to consider the radius of supporting air cover from bases in England, then about 150 miles. Other important elements were the length of the sea crossing; the strength of enemy defences; the availability of suitable beaches; and the proximity of usable ports to help with the build up of men and materiel once the landings had been made. The choice really came down to just four areas: the Pas de Calais, Normandy, the Cotentin Peninsula and Brittany. Many commanders favoured the short sea crossing to the Pas de Calais. However, the enemy had also recognised that this area was an obvious target for an assault and the German defences in the Pas de Calais were the most formidable along the whole of the Channel. Morgan and his staff quickly rejected the Pas de Calais as being unsuitable, choosing Normandy instead.

CAEN THE KEY

In the original plan for the invasion submitted by COSSAC in late 1943, only two British and two American divisions were to land by sea on beaches code-named 'Omaha', 'Gold' and 'Juno'. This number was raised after Eisenhower and Montgomery studied the scheme and decided that the proposed attack was to be made on too narrow a front. They suggested two further beaches and proposed that two more divisions should land; one American division on the eastern base of the Cotentin Peninsular, and one British division closer to Ouistreham.

This new British beach was designated 'Sword Beach' and it stretched from St Aubin sur Mer in the west to the mouth of the River Orne in the east. Eight miles up the Orne was the city of Caen, and from the city a network of roads radiated, linking it to all parts of Normandy. The quick capture of Caen, therefore, became of strategic importance in order to give the Allied landings a swift route into the heartland of

RAF ground crews 'bombing up' a Typhoon fighter-bomber with rocket projectiles. The presence of these aircraft in the sky over Normandy, ready to pounce on German targets with devastating effect, gave the Allies a great tactical advantage. Their great firepower enabled them to interdict large troop movements and severely restrict the mobility of Panzer forces. (Imperial War Museum, CL157)

France. The inclusion of Sword Beach in the invasion plans now made it possible to contemplate seizing Caen on the first day of the landings, before the enemy could mobilise to prevent the city falling to the Allies. Montgomery made it clear that the seizure of Caen was a D-Day objective of the highest order.

To protect Sword Beach and the whole left flank of the landings, it was also decided that an airborne landing would take place to the east of the River Orne during the night before the invasion. This threat to the east of Caen would inevitably split the enemy defences and allow easier progress towards the city.

CHRONOLOGY

1943

April Generalmajor Wilhelm Richter takes command of German 716th Infantry Division and assumes responsibility for the defence of 21 miles of coastline either side of the Orne estuary in Normandy, covering the area designated 'Sword Beach' by the Allies.

23 April Lieutenant-General Morgan appointed to head COSSAC (Chief of Staff to the Supreme Allied Commander) to plan for the invasion of mainland Europe.

2 May Major-General Richard Gale appointed to raise and command British 6th Airborne Division for the invasion of Europe.

July COSSAC produces a report that identifies the area of Normandy between the Orne River and the Cotentin Peninsula as the proposed site for the invasion that was later code-named 'Overlord'.

5 November Generalfeldmarschall Erwin Rommel is appointed to inspect Germany's defensive capacity on the western European coast and to work out defence plans to counter an invasion. Building work on coastal fortifications takes on a new intensity.

December Lieutenant-General Dwight D. Eisenhower is appointed as Supreme Commander for Operation Overlord. General Sir Bernard Montgomery is given command of 21st Army Group, which contains all the land forces that will be used in the invasion.

12 December Major-General Rennie takes command of British 3rd Division for the invasion of Europe.

A Derelict Landing Craft Assault (LCA) lying close to the beach many years after the invasion. These wooden vessels, which had a top speed of just six knots and were vulnerable to all types of enemy fire, carried 30 fully loaded troops from the Landing Ships Infantry (LSI) anchored six miles offshore to the beaches. (Ken Ford)

1944

January Eisenhower and Montgomery decide that Morgan's plan lacks strength and propose that two further landing beaches be added to the assault, one in the American sector on the eastern side of the Cotentin Peninsula, code-named 'Utah', and one in the British sector close to the mouth of the River Orne at Ouistreham, code-named 'Sword'

7 April General Montgomery presents the detailed plan of Overlord to Prime Minister Churchill, King George VI and to all air, naval and ground commanders at St Paul's School in London.British 3rd Division moves south to Hampshire from its training ground in Scotland and undertakes exercises in the Channel.

April British 6th Airborne Division begins its concentration in camps close to the airfields from where its forces will leave for France.

8 May The date of the invasion, D-Day, is fixed for Monday 5 June.

26 May Troops of the British 3rd Division are sealed in their camps and briefing begins on their role in the invasion. French francs and phrase books are issued, last minute preparations made and detailed models of the landing beaches inspected.

3 June British 3rd Division leaves its camps and begins embarkation onto ships that will take it to France.

4 June Bad weather is predicted in the Channel for 5 June and so the invasion is postponed until the following day.

5 June Force S, the invasion fleet destined to land on Sword Beach, sets sail for France from the ports of Portsmouth and Southampton.

5 June, 2256hrs British 6th Airborne Division's advance parties and Major Howard's *coup de main* party take off from airfields in southern England as the spearhead of the invasion.

6 June D-Day

A Landing Craft Flak (LCF) in the Channel during rehearsals for the invasion. The craft carried four 2pdr. and eight 20mm guns and provided protection for assault forces against close-range air or E-boat attack. (Imperial War Museum, A 23758)

0016hrs The first glider of Maj Howard's force touches down in Normandy close to the bridge over the Caen Canal at Benouville and signals the start of the Allied liberation of Normandy. Within 15 minutes, the canal bridge and the nearby bridge over the Orne River are both captured intact.

0050hrs Main body of paratroops lands east of the River Orne.

0300hrs Allied air forces begin their final aerial bombardment of the Atlantic Wall defences prior to the landings.

0320hrs Major-General Gale, together with his headquarters, arrives in Normandy with the main glider landings, which bring with them the heavy weapons of the division.

0330hrs Naval Force S and the shore bombardment fleet arrive off the coast of Normandy.

Dawn British 6th Airborne Division consolidates its gains and secures a lodgement in France: its eastern flank has been secured by the blowing of the bridges over the

In warm spring sunshine, commandos of the 1st Special Service Brigade receive a detailed briefing from their officer in one of the assembly camps close to Southampton. (Imperial War Museum, H38948)

River Dives between Caen and the sea; the German gun battery at Merville to the north of the landings has been destroyed; the bridges over the Orne River and Caen Canal have been captured; and the villages marking the southern perimeter of the airborne landings have been seized.

0530hrs Troops begin to disembark from the transport ships that carried them over the Channel, into assault craft that will take them to the landing sites on Sword Beach, Queen Red and White sectors.

0600hrs Naval bombardment of German coast defences and gun batteries begins.

0725hrs Assault companies of 8th Brigade, part of British 3rd Division, land on Queen Red and White beaches. They are supported by armour of 27th Armoured Brigade and the specialised tanks from 79th Armoured Division. They then begin the struggle to overcome the enemy and exit the beaches.

Entrance into the underground complex known to the Germans as Wiederstandsnest 17 (Wn 17) and to the British as strongpoint Hillman. The fortified underground position, measuring 400yds by 600yds was located just to the south-east of Colleville, about two miles from Sword Beach. It was captured on D-Day by 1st Suffolks. (Ken Ford

The Caen Canal at Benouville today, with the new lifting-bridge spanning the waterway. The Café Gondrée is in the background on the other side of the canal. In the foreground is the original 5cm gun captured along with the bridge during the first minutes of D-Day, although it is not in its original gun pit. The whole site was rearranged when the new bridge was installed in 1994. (Ken Ford)

0800hrs The first of Brigadier Lord Lovat's commandos arrive over Queen Beach when 4 Commando comes ashore to attack the gun batteries at Ouistreham and the Casino at Riva Bella.

0830hrs 8th Brigade are clear of the beaches and begin moving inland towards Hermanville.

1000hrs 185th Brigade, 3rd Division's intermediate brigade, begin to come ashore, along with more tanks from 27th Armoured Brigade, and begin their drive to capture Caen.

1300hrs 9th Brigade, 3rd Division's reserve brigade, lands over Sword Beach and starts its drive on Caen, but it is soon thrown into some disarray by the loss of its commander.

1310hrs British 1st Special Service Brigade arrives from Sword Beach to link up with the 6th Airborne Division at the Benouville bridges.

1500hrs 3rd Division's advance on Caen begins to falter when 1st Suffolks get bogged down clearing the Morris and Hillman strongpoints

1600hrs German 21st Panzer Division launches a counter-attack against the landings and immediately runs into the 1st King's Shropshire Light Infantry supported by tanks of the Staffordshire Yeomanry.

1900hrs After losing many tanks during the advance, elements of 21st Panzer Division reach the sea between Lion and Luc sur Mer, but few reinforcements arrive to help the enemy exploit the gap between Sword Beach and the Canadian landings on Juno Beach.

2100hrs 6th Airlanding Brigade arrive by gliders to join the remainder of British 6th Airborne Division and set down on Landing Zone W, west of the Orne. The descent of hundreds of aircraft over the German armoured troops causes some panic at its HQ and 21st Panzer Division is withdrawn back onto the high ground north of Caen, where it digs in for the night.

2400hrs With their drive on Caen stalled, 3rd Division's three brigades consolidate their gains and make ready for a resumption of the advance the next day.

OPPOSING COMMANDERS

I n December 1943 the Supreme Commander for Operation Overlord was appointed. The two most powerful and able soldiers in the American and British armies at that time, General George C. Marshall, US Army Chief-of-Staff and General Sir Alan Brooke, Chief of the Imperial General Staff, were considered for the post, but both were passed over. Marshall was considered indispensable to Roosevelt, and Brooke was overlooked because he was British. With most of the effort in Europe both on D-Day and in the subsequent push into Germany being provided by the Americans, it was politic that the Supreme Commander should be from the USA. **General Dwight D. Eisenhower** was appointed to the post in recognition of his successes in North Africa, Sicily and Italy. By then he had commanded three amphibious invasions and was well respected by numerous important political and military figures. Eisenhower exercised notable diplomatic skills, and he was probably the only prominent senior commander who could pull the disparate groups of different nationalities and services that made up the Allied forces together into one coherent team.

General Sir Bernard Montgomery, Commander 21st Army Group, was not content with COSSAC's original plans for the invasion, suggesting that it lacked overall strength. He and Gen Eisenhower decided to add two further divisions to the assault and insisted on an extra landing beach, Sword Beach. (Ken Ford)

ALLIED COMMANDERS

The appointees to all three of the subordinate commands and the deputy commander for the invasion were all British. **General Sir Bernard Montgomery** was placed in command of all the land forces in 21st Army Group for the actual assault, both British and American. He would retain control until such time that Eisenhower could take overall command in the field. Admiral Sir Bertram Ramsay headed the Allied Naval Expeditionary Force and Air Chief Marshal Sir Trafford Leigh Mallory was appointed to lead the Allied Expeditionary Air Force. The Deputy Supreme Commander was Air Chief Marshal Sir Arthur Tedder.

For the assault on Normandy, Montgomery's 21st Army Group consisted of two armies; US 1st Army, commanded by Lieutenant-General Omar Bradley, and British 2nd Army, commanded by **Lieutenant-General Sir Miles Dempsey**. Both generals had a wealth of field experience as corps commanders in North Africa and the Mediterranean. Bradley's two corps were to land in the American sector close to the base of the Cotentin Peninsula either side of the estuary of the River Vire. US VII Corps, commanded by Major-General Collins, would land on the beach code-named 'Utah', and US V Corps, commanded by Major-General Gerow, would land on 'Omaha'. Dempsey likewise was to land two corps in the British sector: **Lieutenant-General John Crocker** would command I Corps on 'Gold' beach, and XXX Corps, commanded by Lieutenant-General Gerard Bucknall, would land on 'Juno' and 'Sword' beaches.

HT **British D-Day commanders:** en John Crocker of I Corps; en Miles Dempsey, 2nd Army; LtGen Gerard Bucknall, Corps. (Imperial War eum, B5325)

jor-General Richard Gale sed and commanded British Airborne Division ready for invasion of Europe. The most ccessful of all of the D-Day nerals, his division gained all its objectives and remained in line until August 1944. iperial War Museum, B 5352)

ajor-General Tom Rennie, mmander of British 3rd vision, talks to a tank crew m 27th Armoured Brigade ior to embarkation at Gosport. iperial War Museum, H39002)

Bucknall had commanded the British 5th Division in Sicily and Italy and Crocker had led the British IX Corps in Tunisia before they were both given new corps commands for the invasion.

Sword Beach was the objective of **Major-General Tom Rennie's** British 3rd Division. Rennie had been a battalion commander at El Alamein and later headed a brigade of the Highland Division in Sicily. In December 1943 he was promoted to major-general and ordered back to England to take over the 3rd Division and train it specifically for the invasion.

Also at the disposal of Dempsey's British 2nd Army was the 6th Airborne Division, commanded by **Major-General Richard Gale**. Gale had served for 17 years in India after the First World War and had then been appointed to various staff posts at the War Office. In August 1941 he took command of 1st Parachute Brigade and began a programme of rigorous training. In the spring of the following year he was recalled to the War Office once again, but left in April 1943 to raise the 6th Airborne Division and prepare it for the invasion.

GERMAN COMMANDERS

The area of Normandy destined to receive the great Allied assault was in the sector defended by the German Seventh Army, commanded by **Generaloberst Friedrich Dollmann**. Dollmann's army reported to **Generalfeldmarschall Erwin Rommel** as part of his Army Group B, which in turn came under the command of **Generalfeldmarschall Gerd von Rundstedt**, Commander-in-Chief (West).

Generaloberst Friedrich Dollmann had been in command of Seventh Army since the outbreak of war in 1939. Seventh Army had played a small part in the German capture of France in 1940. Since then, Dollman and his army had garrisoned the western half of France, carrying out occupation duties for almost four years. As a result, Dollmann had gradually lost touch with developments in his field, and

15

he had little grasp of armoured warfare or the tactical use of air power. When the Allied blow came, his reactions were slow and often erratic, allowing the Allies more freedom of movement than they expected.

General der Artillerie Erich Marcks, commander of German LXXXIV Corps, controlled the divisions manning the Normandy beaches. In June 1944 his corps stood in the centre of the landing operations. Marcks had seen service in Poland in 1939 and had commanded a division in Russia. He was wounded in June 1941 and lost his left leg. However, his injuries did not harm his military career. In August 1943 he was assigned to LXXXIV Corps in Normandy, and given the task of defending 240 miles of coastline between the Orne estuary and St Malo with six divisions.

Opposite Sword Beach and astride the River Orne, Marcks had the German 716th Infantry Division holding 21 miles of coastline onto which the British and Canadian forces would descend. This division was headed by **Generalleutnant Wilhelm Richter**, an artillery officer and a veteran of action in Poland, Belgium and Russia.

Many miles inland, but also in the sector opposite Sword Beach astride the River Orne, was the German 21st Panzer Division, commanded by **Generalmajor Edgar Feuchtinger**. This Panzer unit was under the control of GFM Rommel's Army Group B and was located as a mobile reserve, able to strike anywhere in Normandy that an Allied landing might take place. Feuchtinger had fought in the campaigns in the Netherlands, Belgium and France in 1940 as an artillery regimental commander, and he was later wounded in Russia at the siege of Leningrad in August 1942. Although he had no experience of armoured units, he was given command of a reformed 21st Panzer Division in August 1943. He gained his promotion as a result of political connections, having been a Nazi Party organiser in the 1930s and a friend of Hitler. He was, however, not an inspired choice, and his performance as leader of the 21st Panzer Division was later called into question when he was court-martialled in March 1945.

OPPOSING ARMIES

THE BRITISH ARMY

The British formations that led the invasion of Normandy on 6 June 1944 were well trained, well equipped, well supported and well led. Their morale was sky high. Since the defeat in France in 1940, which had forced the evacuation of its Expeditionary Force from Dunkirk, there had been revolutionary changes in Britain's fighting arms. The British Army's return to France was made by units that had learned much from the actions of other divisions in theatres all over the world.

One such division was the **3rd Infantry Division**, which was destined to land on Sword Beach. In 1940, commanded by Montgomery, it had been evacuated out of Dunkirk and arrived back in England after fighting many fierce rearguard actions against the advancing Germans. All of its equipment and transport was left in France. The 3rd Division was completely re-equipped and spent the next four years training and preparing itself for a return to war. It was earmarked for several campaigns, including the invasion of Sicily, but remained at home whilst other divisions achieved fame in North Africa and Italy. In the summer of 1943 its then commander, Major-General Ramsden, secured an undertaking that the 3rd Division would lead the British return to north-west Europe and that it would be the first division ashore. From then on, all training assumed a new focus and Ramsden's division entered a programme of preparation that was both vigorous and realistic, concentrating on amphibious assaults and attacks on fixed strongpoints.

A Landing Craft Gun Large, LCG (L), on passage in the Solent passing Hurst Castle. The craft, which carried two 4in. guns and two 20mm cannon, provided close-support fire during the run-in of the assault waves to the landing beaches. Its larger guns had a range of over eight miles, so it was also able to give indirect fire support to troops moving inland. (Imperial War Museum, A23754)

The division quickly built up a close relationship with the Royal Navy and began a series of exercises up and down the coast of Scotland. In late 1943 it joined with the naval force that would carry it to the Normandy beaches. Known as Task Force S and commanded by Rear Admiral A.G. Talbot, it was responsible for the seaborne element of the landings on Sword Beach.

In December 1943, Montgomery was appointed head of 21st Army Group and designated land commander for the invasion. He immediately brought in new commanders for some of the units already allocated to Overlord, appointing officers who had previously fought with him in North Africa and in the Mediterranean and in whom he had confidence. In the 3rd Division Ramsden was replaced by MajGen Tom Rennie, an 8th Army veteran who had commanded a brigade in Sicily.

The British 3rd Infantry Division consisted of three brigades, 8th, 9th and 185th, each containing three battalions. The 8th Brigade consisted of 1st Suffolk Regiment, 2nd East Yorkshire Regiment and 1st South Lancashire Regiment; the 9th Brigade contained 2nd Lincolnshire Regiment, 1st King's Own Scottish Borderers (KOSB) and 2nd Royal Ulster Rifles; and the 185th Brigade was made up of 2nd Royal Warwickshire Regiment, 1st Royal Norfolk Regiment and 2nd Shropshire Light Infantry. In addition, the division had the usual complement of support troops – 3rd Reconnaissance Regiment RAC, 3rd Divisional Engineers and 3rd Divisional Signals. Heavy machine-gun and mortar support was provided by 2nd Middlesex Regiment.

The 3rd Division's artillery element (7th, 33rd and 76th Field Regiments) were re-equipped with self-propelled Priest 105mm howitzers, and its 20th Anti-tank Regiment was given Wolverine 3in. SP guns (US M10s). This conversion to self-propelled artillery increased the speed with which the guns could be disembarked and allowed them to fire from the decks of landing-craft during the run-in to the beaches, thus increasing the artillery support given to the division during the final critical approach to its landing sectors. The 92nd Light Anti-aircraft Regiment RA completed the heavy firepower of the division.

Joining with Rennie's division were a number of other units that were placed under command specifically for the assault. These specialised forces included an armoured element in the shape of 27th Armoured Brigade and 5th Assault Regiment Royal Engineers (from 79th Armoured Division); heavier firepower from the guns of 53rd Medium Regiment Royal Artillery; and the swift mobility of Lord Lovat's 1st Special Service Brigade, comprising 3, 4, 6 and 45 (Royal Marine) Commandos. To these were added units to organise the beach landings and traffic movement out of the beachhead – 101st Beach Area and Port Operating Group. To protect from enemy interference from the air, two more anti-aircraft regiments were added. Two specialist field engineer companies were also allocated to help with demolitions and obstacle clearance, while a host of other minor service units took care of various fine details associated with the amphibious landings. All these new arrivals resulted in a doubling in the size of the division, and with these changes and additions the British 3rd Infantry Division became the most powerful division that had ever left England.

The British **6th Airborne Division** was given the task of landing east of the River Orne prior to the seaborne landings, in order to protect the left flank of the invasion forces. The division was raised on 2 May 1943 under the command of Major-General Richard Gale, with the specific role of providing airborne troops to assist any invasion against occupied Europe. The division was, therefore, completely new, and it had just one year to train and ready itself for this momentous task. It comprised three brigades - 3rd and 5th Parachute Brigades and 6th Airlanding Brigade - each containing three battalions. The 3rd Parachute Brigade consisted of 8th and 9th Battalions the Parachute Regiment and 1st Canadian

Parachute Battalion; the 5th Parachute Brigade consisted of 7th, 12t and 13th Battalions the Parachute Regiment; and the 6th Airlandin Brigade was made up of 12th Devonshire Regiment, 2nd Oxfordshir and Buckinghamshire Light Infantry and 1st Royal Ulster Rifles. Th 53rd Airlanding Light Regiment Royal Artillery provided artiller support, whilst 6th Airborne Armoured Reconnaissance Regiment RAC 6th Airborne Divisional Engineers and 6th Airborne Divisional Signa gave specialist support.

THE GERMAN ARMY

At the time of the landings, there were 60 German divisions in the Wes waiting for the Allies to strike. It sounds like an impressively large forc but these divisions were manning a coastline that stretched fror Denmark to the Spanish border. They also guarded the Frenc Mediterranean coast, as well as garrisoning the interior of the occupie territories of France, Belgium, Holland and Denmark. Of these division 20 were static formations, raised to hold a sector of the coast and no easily moved since they lacked any significant transport of their own Many of the armoured units in France and Belgium in early 1944 ha only arrived from the East in the spring after much heavy fighting. The suffered severe shortages of manpower and equipment and used th posting to the West to rebuild their strength. The bulk of these Panze outfits were stationed in the strategically important central area betwee Holland and the mouth of the Seine, and they were unable to interfer with the landings in Normandy, except after an appreciable delay.

The German army of occupation in France was increasingl hampered by the destruction of its internal communications by Allie bombing and acts of sabotage committed by the French Resistance Roads, railways, rivers, canals and depots were, by June 1944, in a ver poor state, and their condition severely restricted the transportation o fuel and supplies. Open movement of military convoys becam increasingly difficult as the date of the invasion approached, especiall as a result of the strafing tactics employed by low-flying British an American fighter-bombers. The Allied dominance of the air meant tha few massed troop movements could be undertaken in daylight, furthe restricting Germany's ability to react quickly to the Allied landings.

The sector that included Sword Beach and the drop zone of th British 6th Airborne Division was held by a single German division **716th Infantry Division**. The 716th was originally activated under th command of Oberst Otto Matterstock on 2 May 1941 from replacemen units raised in Military District VI at Munster. Its soldiers were older me from the Rhineland and Westphalia area. The 716th was one of th 15 static divisions raised in Mobilisation Wave 15, beginning in Apri 1941, which was specifically organised for occupation and anti-invasio duties in the West and in the Balkans. It was immediately sent to th Caen area for coastal defence duties and, after a brief spell in Soisson and Belgium, returned once again to Normandy in June 1942, where i remained until D-Day.

Initially the division consisted of two regiments, 726th and 736t Infantry Regiments, each with three battalions. Its artillery support wa provided by 656th Artillery Battalion, containing three batteries of field guns, but this was later supplemented by the arrival of an additional battalion, and the division's artillery unit was upgraded and redesignated 1716th Artillery Regiment. Being a static formation, the division was without any vehicles for troop movements and what little transport it did have was often horse-drawn.

It was inevitable that the division's static role on the Normandy coastline would be seen as a source of manpower to help make up the German losses in Russia, and many of its soldiers were drafted to the East, to be replaced by lower quality troops from the occupied territories of Poland and Russia. Little by little, the division's strength and morale was diluted by the influx of foreign soldiers drafted in under the threat of service to the German Army or brutal captivity in concentration camps.

In April 1943 Generalmajor (later Generalleutnant) Wilhelm Richter arrived to take over the division. His task was to improve the defences and secure the area against invasion, and his responsibility was to hold a front of over 21 miles of coastline. It was a demanding task, particularly when one considers that a good division could reasonably be expected to hold only six miles of front. Richter complained that his forces were 'beaded along the coast like a string of pearls'. The division did, however, have some assistance to help stiffen its defensive role, sited as it was behind the much vaunted, but still incomplete, concrete emplacements and defences of the Atlantic Wall. Richter set his men to help in the construction of the coast defences and assisted in organising over 40 fortified centres of resistance in his sector.

As anticipation of an Allied invasion grew, Richter was reinforced by two battalions of *Osttruppen* from the occupied territories of the Soviet Union. These Eastern troops were complete units of about 1,000 men, and one battalion was assigned to each of the regiments – 441st East Battalion went to 726th Regiment and 642nd East Battalion joined 736th Regiment. The *Osttruppen* acted as the fourth battalion for each unit, although their usefulness was considered suspect, as were similar battalions placed in the line elsewhere along the French coastline. As one senior German general scathingly observed: 'It is hard to imagine why Russians should fight for the Germans, in France against Americans.'

When the Allied blow struck, the German 716th Division became involved in fighting against not only the British at Sword Beach and the 6th Airborne east of the Orne, but also against the Canadians on Juno Beach. Approximately half of the division's strength was dispersed between the two sectors. In the area of Sword Beach, Richter had the first and second battalions of 736th Regiment holding the coastline, with its third battalion inland acting as a reserve. The Regiment's 642nd East Battalion was dispersed behind the coast, mainly in the area east of the Orne.

The armour readily available to counter the landings near Caen amounted to just one division, **21st Panzer Division**, which had its headquarters at St Pierre sur Dives, about 20 miles south-west of Caen. There were other Panzer units allocated to resist an invasion along the Normandy coast, but they were stationed well inland, waiting to see where the Allied blow would land. The 12th SS Panzer Division 'Hitler

Generalmajor Edgar Feuchtinger, commander of German 21st Panzer Division, had fought in the campaigns of 1940 and in Russia, where he was wounded during the siege of Leningrad in August 1942. His division carried out the only major counter-attack against the Allied landings on D-Day.
(Bundesarchiv, 87/120/19A)

German troops mine a bridge over the Dives Canal before the invasion. The River Dives marked the eastern boundary of the proposed landings of British 6th Airborne Division. (Bundesarchiv, 721/382/32A)

Jugend' was close to Lisieux and the Panzer Lehr Division was in the Chartres area, both within a day's march of Caen. In addition, the 17th SS Panzergrenadier Division south of Tours, the 2nd Panzer Division east of the Seine and 116th Panzer Division near Paris could all arrive in the area of the invasion within a matter of days.

The 21st Panzer Division was commanded by Generalmajor Edgar Feuchtinger. It was available for immediate counter-attack wherever it was required in Normandy and was under the control of Army Group B. By contrast, the 12th SS Panzer and Panzer Lehr Divisions were part of the strategic reserve and could only be released by authority of the Supreme Commander, Adolf Hitler. The Führer needed to be convinced that any landing, no matter where it might fall along the Channel coast, was the main invasion and not just a feint to draw off his mobile forces whilst other larger landings took place elsewhere. The German Supreme Command felt sure that the Allies would land in the Pas de Calais and even weeks after the Normandy landings they still expected that fresh assaults would be made in that area.

The 21st Panzer Division was a reconstituted division organised after the original unit was destroyed in Tunisia in May 1943. It was formed at Rennes in July 1943 from veterans of the Eastern front and those soldiers of the Africa Corps who had escaped the disaster in Tunisia, together with some from miscellaneous units of the German Seventh Army. These latter troops were often other people's rejects and not always the best of men. General Leo Geyr von Schweppenburg had commented that the 21st Panzers were flawed because they were composed of many undesirable personnel with bad traits, which even thorough and experienced training could never overcome.

The division was composed of 100th Panzer Regiment and the 125th and 192nd Panzergrenadier Regiments, all of which had two battalions instead of the normal three. The 155th Panzer Artillery Regiment; the 21st Panzer Reconnaissance Battalion, the 220th Panzer Pioneer Battalion and the 305th Anti-aircraft Battalion completed the make-up of this division. Raised in France, its transport was composed mainly of captured French vehicles and it was armed with many obsolete weapons. Its tanks were mostly PzKpfw IVs together with some light tanks of foreign manufacture. Of the ten Panzer and Panzergrenadier divisions in the West in early 1944, the 21st Panzer Division was the only one rated as unfit for service in Russia.

In the air, the German Luftwaffe was only a shadow of the force that had waged war on Britain in 1940. Most of its strength was either engaged in Russia, or committed against the Allied bombing effort that was pounding the industries and cities of the Reich on a daily basis. The German Third Air Force (Luftflotte 3), commanded by Generalfeldmarschall Hugo Sperrle, was responsible for air attacks against any Allied invasion. The Third Air Force covered the whole of France, Holland and Belgium. However, to protect this massive area it had only 168 Messerschmitt Bf 109 and Focke-Wulf Fw 190 fighters in II Fighter Corps, and it had just 67 Focke-Wulf Fw 190F fighter-bombers in II Air Corps to provide air support for ground troops. Nor were all of these aircraft airworthy, with the average unit serviceability at below 50 per cent. They were also short of experienced air crews and adequate fuel stocks.

At sea, the German Navy had also been curtailed in its offensive capability through the superiority of Allied air and sea power. Admiral Theodore Kranke, Commander-in-Chief Naval Group Command West, was responsible for opposing the invasion, but he had few craft in the western Channel with which to counter it. The only vessels that were available in the area on 6 June between Boulogne and Cherbourg were three torpedo boats, one minesweeper, 29 S-boats (small, fast motor torpedo boats), 36 R-boats (motor minesweepers), 35 auxiliary minesweepers and patrol boats, 11 gun carriers and three mine-laying craft. This was all that Kranke had to counter an Allied naval force of over 6,000 vessels.

OPPOSING PLANS

A Horsa glider, which displays the three broad white recognition stripes of the Allies, is towed skywards by an Armstrong Whitworth Albemarle tug aircraft. (Imperial War Museum, H39183)

Operation Overlord provided for ten divisions to be put ashore in Normandy on 6 June. Eight of these divisions would land as assault waves, whilst the other two would come ashore as part of the build-up of forces later that day. On the American front, two airborne divisions would land during the hours of darkness in the early morning and seize the land behind their beaches, whilst just after daylight three divisions would land on Utah and Omaha beaches either side of the estuary of the River Vire. British and Canadian forces would land one airborne division just after midnight to secure the eastern flank, and three divisions would then come ashore on beaches Gold, Juno and Sword during the early morning.

6th Airborne's Targets

Major-General Richard Gale's 6th Airborne Division had been set a series of tasks aimed at protecting the eastern flank of the seaborne landings and providing of a firm lodgement from which a rapid expansion of the beachhead could be launched when the time was right. Gale had been ordered to seize the bridges over the River Orne and the Caen Canal at Bénouville to allow a link-up between the beaches and the airborne forces. He had also been tasked with destroying the bridges over the River Dives between Caen and the sea to prevent German counter-attacks from the east, and to hold the ground in between the Orne and Dives rivers in order to deny it to the enemy. In addition, the gun battery at Merville had to be eliminated before it could interfere with the seaborne landings. Several drop zones (DZs) for paratroops

...mmandos from 1st Special
...rvice Brigade embark onto
...I (S) – Landing Craft Infantry
...nall – at Warsash in
...uthampton Water. These small
...aft would take the commandos
...ross the Channel and set them
...wn right onto the landing
...aches. The vessels could carry
...fully equipped troops below
...ck. Disembarkation was via
...ur ramps manhandled over bow
...onsons. (Imperial War
...useum, H39043)

and landing zones (LZs) for gliders had been allocated to receive units of the 6th Airborne. The 5th Parachute Brigade was to land on DZ 'N' north of Ranville; 3rd Parachute Brigade was given DZ 'V' to the north-east near Varaville; 8th Parachute Battalion (from 3rd Parachute Brigade) was to land separately on DZ 'K' to the south-east near Touffréville, whilst the *coup de main* parties assaulting Bénouville were to land on LZ 'X' and 'Y' close to the bridges. A further landing zone, LZ 'W', was identified on the western side of the Caen Canal near St Aubin to receive the division's follow-up brigade, 6th Airlanding Brigade, who would land in gliders on the evening of D-Day. The brigade could not be brought over to Normandy sooner because, owing to a lack of aircraft, it had to wait until the towing aircraft used during the assault phase had returned to England and been made ready for a second mission.

Sword Beach and the area to the east of the River Orne marked the left-hand section of the British seaborne assault. Just offshore of Sword Beach, most notably opposite Lion sur Mer, were large shoals that made the approach to the beaches difficult. These shallows influenced the actual landfall of the assault waves and a decision was made that the initial landings would take place in the locality of the seaside hamlet of La Brèche. The targeted area had a clear approach from the sea and good access inland, but it was, unfortunately, only wide enough to land one brigade at a time.

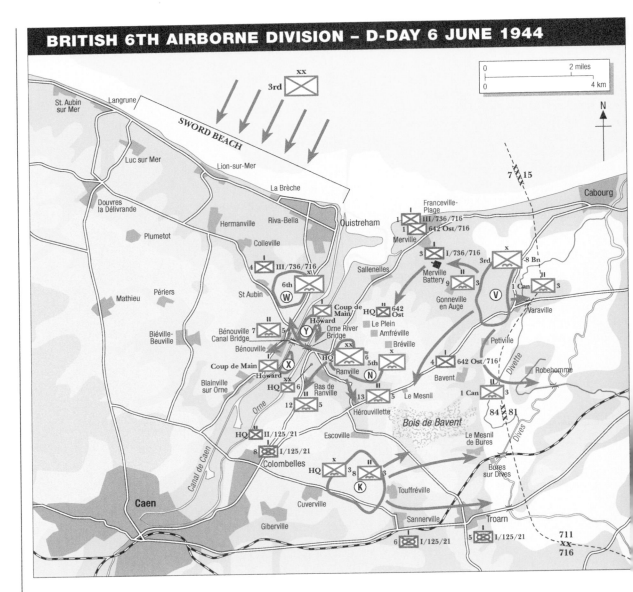

Sword Beach was itself composed of four sectors, which were code-named 'Oboe', 'Peter', 'Queen' and 'Roger'. These sectors were in turn divided up into three areas ('Green', 'White' and 'Red'), which represented right-hand, central and left-hand parts of each beach respectively. The proposed landing site on Sword Beach at La Brèche was in the designated Queen Red and Queen White sectors.

With the landing site identified and confirmed, Allied planners could now concentrate on how they might best gain a secure foothold on the beaches. For the German planners, their problem was much more difficult: they did not know when or where the blow might fall on the hundreds of miles of occupied coastline that they were defending. They had to prepare for all eventualities.

The German Defensive Plan

The German plan of defence against an Allied invasion was built around

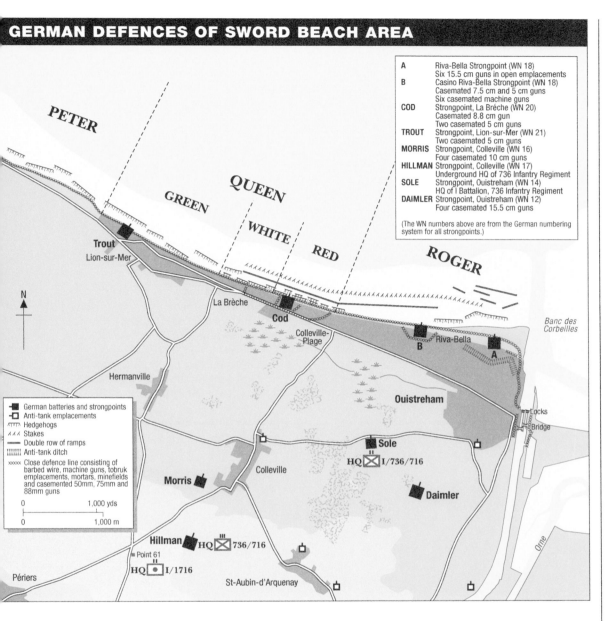

A	Riva-Bella Strongpoint (WN 18)
	Six 15.5 cm guns in open emplacements
B	Casino Riva-Bella Strongpoint (WN 18)
	Casemated 7.5 cm and 5 cm guns
	Six casemated machine guns
COD	Strongpoint, La Brèche (WN 20)
	Casemated 8.8 cm gun
	Two casemated 5 cm guns
TROUT	Strongpoint, Lion-sur-Mer (WN 21)
	Two casemated 5 cm guns
MORRIS	Strongpoint, Colleville (WN 16)
	Four casemated 10 cm guns
HILLMAN	Strongpoint, Colleville (WN 17)
	Underground HQ of 736 Infantry Regiment
SOLE	Strongpoint, Ouistreham (WN 14)
	HQ of I Battalion, 736 Infantry Regiment
DAIMLER	Strongpoint, Ouistreham (WN 12)
	Four casemated 15.5 cm guns

(The WN numbers above are from the German numbering system for all strongpoints.)

German batteries and strongpoints
Anti-tank emplacements
Hedgehogs
Stakes
Double row of ramps
Anti-tank ditch
Close defence line consisting of barbed wire, machine guns, tobruk emplacements, mortars, minefields and casemented 50mm, 75mm and 88mm guns

0   1,000 yds
0   1,000 m

two key principles. First, the assaulting forces must be stopped or disorganised along the waterline itself by impregnable fixed defences and, second, they must be destroyed by an armoured counter-attack, either on the exposed beaches, or on suitable ground inland. This latter point provoked prolonged and bitter debate, dividing the Germans into two schools of thought. Rommel proposed that the armoured attack against an invasion must be made whilst the invaders were actually in the process of landing, just at the time they were most vulnerable. He reasoned that Panzer divisions must, therefore, be located close to the coast ready for action on the same day that the landings occurred. Geyr von Schweppenburg, commander Panzer Army West, and von Rundstedt, Commander-in-Chief (West) did not agree, claiming that the best option was to attack the Allied invaders with an overwhelming armoured force, on ground suitable for such tactics to be employed. Rommel was certain that Allied air superiority would foil any such attempt to mass Panzer divisions and that such a policy would be doomed to failure. He went so far as to suggest that if the Allies managed to establish a beachhead then the war would have been lost. Hitler, to whom all such arguments were referred for a decision, fudged the issue. He compromised, allowing one Panzer division to be located close to the coast under Army Group B's control for immediate use, whilst keeping others under his express control further back. In Normandy the compromise resulted in 21st Panzer Division being located south of Caen, and 12th SS Panzer Division 'Hitler Jugend' and Panzer Lehr Division being held further away, more than 100 miles from the Channel.

The main defence against invasion rested in the strength of the Atlantic Wall, a line of interlocking concrete defensive stongpoints and minefields stretching along the Channel coastline. Construction of these defences began in 1941 but progressed at a very slow pace whilst Hitler's forces achieved a succession of victories elsewhere. When things started to go seriously wrong for Germany and the great empire of the Third Reich began to contract, building work on the fortification of the Channel coast quickened in pace. In late 1943, Rommel was appointed to investigate and improve the strength and location of the fortifications. He ordered the upgrading of all existing building work and an increase in the numbers and location of a range of new fortifications. His determined approach and strategic eye for detail enabled a remarkable strengthening of the Atlantic Wall in a very short time, but when the Allied invasion came ashore in June 1944 its effectiveness was still well short of what had originally been planned.

Along the length of Sword Beach, however, the Atlantic Wall offered a significant obstacle to the Allied forces. General Richter, commander of the German division garrisoning this stretch of coastline, had added his improvements to Rommel's defensive plan and created a number of interlocking strongpoints to supplement the wall of fortifications.

The first thing that the invasion craft would meet on their run-in to Sword Beach was the fire of long-range artillery. The landing beaches were within range of the heavy guns of batteries away to the east as far afield as Le Havre, with calibres of 5.9–15.0in. Closer to Sword Beach were the smaller artillery positions at Merville, Ouistreham, Riva Bella and Colleville, housing guns with calibres of 4.1–6.1in. Next on their approach to the beaches the landing-craft would hit underwater defences, which were placed between high- and low-water marks and consisted of stakes topped by mines, steel obstacles called 'hedgehogs' made from sections of railway line, mined rafts floating just under the water, steel ramps and minefields. Once they had managed to manoeuvre themselves past these obstacles, the landing-craft would finally hit the beach. Here they would come under fire from the interlocking machine-gun posts, mortar weapons pits and anti-tank pill boxes, whose fire would be sweeping the area. Behind this line of fortifications were anti-tank sea walls, barbed wire entanglements and more minefields.

'Hobart's Funnies'

The 5th Assault Regiment, from 79th Armoured Division, that was to land in support of 3rd Division had specialised armour in its arsenal with

ich to overcome these obstacles. Major-General Percy Hobart, the
ovative commander of 79th Armoured Division, had gathered
ether a variety of special tanks each with a specific purpose. All were
igned to attack some particular type of German defence. There were
erman 'Crab' tanks which had a revolving drum attached to their
nt onto which were connected large steel chains. As the drum
ated, the metal chains smashed into the ground exploding any mines
t lay in the tank's path and, thereby, cleared a lane through the
nefield for following vehicles. There were Armoured Vehicles Royal
gineers (AVREs) modified for specific tasks such as bridge -laying,
ing in ditches, crossing anti-tank walls and firing large charges against
ncrete emplacements. Other tanks were modified as flame-thrower
nicles, while 'Bobbin' tanks – Churchills capable of laying flexible
pets to allow the passage of vehicles over sand and shingle – were also
veloped. All of these special types of tanks were at the disposal of
l Division for its assault.

At selected locations along the seafront were strongpoints, which
re built to give mutual support. These were often given individual
de-names by the Allies and specific plans were made for their capture.
ong Sword Beach the fortified areas were: 'Trout' at Lion sur Mer,
od' at La Brèche, the 'Casino' at Riva Bella, and the 'shore battery' at
va Bella/Ouistreham. Inland from the beaches, sited to prevent Allied
rces moving off the beach, were other fortified strongpoints: 'Sole'
uth-west of Ouistreham; 'Daimler' to the south of Ouistreham; and
lorris' and 'Hillman' near Colleville.

The task of transporting Allied forces onto Sword Beach and
fending them from enemy interference during the passage was given to
e ships of the Royal and Commonwealth Navies. Force S, commanded
R/Adm A.G. Talbot, was part of the Eastern Task Force which
pported the British and Canadian beaches of Gold, Juno and Sword.
rce S comprised three Assault Groups, S1, S2 and S3. Assault Group S3
is to be responsible for the initial landing of the assault brigade,
llowed by Group S2 with the intermediate brigade, whilst Group S1
uld take responsibility for the landings of the reserve brigade. Each of
ese naval groups would have their own flotillas of various types of
nding-craft.

Sword Beach, being the easternmost section of the British assault
ea, was seen as the most vulnerable to enemy attack, both from the
eavy guns around Le Havre and from the German vessels based there.
r this reason a powerful bombarding force was to be stationed to port
the invasion convoys, to counter such threats. This force was to
ntain two battleships, a 15in. gun monitor and five cruisers, supported
13 destroyers and numerous other lighter vessels.

The 3rd British Division was to lead the invasion onto Sword Beach
th its 8th Brigade carrying out the initial assault. It would land two
attalions up front, with a reserve battalion following closely behind.
he 1st South Lancashires would touch down on Queen White, whilst
nd East Yorkshires would land on Queen Red and 1st Suffolk Regiment
ould follow them in. All three battalions were to be conveyed ashore in
ny wooden LCAs (Landing Craft Assault), each carrying around
fully laden troops. They would be supported at the same time by DD
Duplex Drive) tanks from the 13th/18th Hussars (27th Armoured

Lieutenants Bob de la Tour, Don Wells, John Vischer and Bob Midwood of 22nd Independent Parachute Company synchronise watches on the evening of 5 June before boarding their aircraft to lead their advance parties into Normandy. (Imperial War Museum, H39070)

Brigade). These DD tanks were amphibious Sherman tanks, canvas screens to provide buoyancy and propelled through the water by two external propellers. They would be launched 5,000yds out at sea and would 'swim' in to the shore so as to arrive just as the leading waves of infantry hit the beach. Their low silhouette in the water would be their best protection during the passage ashore, and it was hoped that it would allow them to get close to the enemy strongpoints without attracting too much heavy fire. Once they touched down, their canvas skirts would be dropped, their propellers disengaged and they would then perform as normal armour. The arrival of these tanks on the beach, coinciding with the arrival of the infantry, would enable enemy strongpoints to be attacked immediately.

Just behind the first wave, and arriving almost simultaneously, specialised armour from 79th Armoured Division would land in LCTs (Landing Craft Tanks) comprising 22nd Dragoons, Westminster Dragoons and 5th Assault Regiment Royal Engineers. These units were tasked with the role of overcoming beach defences, clearing minefields and opening gaps from the beach for the infantry and tanks to pass through.

Next would land the remaining regiments of tanks of 27th Armoured Brigade – 1st East Riding Yeomanry and the Staffordshire Yeomanry – together with the three self-propelled regiments (7th, 33rd and 76th Field Regiments RA) of the 3rd Division's field artillery. These forces would add punch to the 8th Brigade's move inland.

The immediate objectives for the first assaulting waves were to clear the beach of underwater obstacles, silence local defences – especially the German strongpoint 'Cod' just behind the shoreline – and secure exits from the beaches. They were then to move inland and attack their designated objectives in order to leave the beach area relatively clear for the follow-up waves of troops and armour. The 1st South Lancs would press inland to take the village of Hermanville, 2nd East Yorks would move on the two German strongpoints of 'Sole' and 'Daimler' to the west of Ouistreham, whilst the 1st Suffolks would advance through Colleville and attack the enemy strongpoints of 'Morris' and 'Hillman'.

Whilst these units attacked German defences close to the landing sites, other enemy strongpoints would be sure to interfere with the landing. To the east were two such fortified areas; the Casino at Riva Bella and the shore battery on the seafront at Ouistreham. To the west was the strongpoint 'Trout' at Lion sur Mer. Warships would bombard these sites during the early hours after dawn, then 4 Commando (from 1st Special Service Brigade) would land just behind the assault waves and advance inland to capture the eastern strongpoints from the rear. At the same time, 41 Royal Marine Commando (from 4th Special Service Brigade) would move to the west to attack 'Trout'.

After the first waves had gained a foothold, other groups would arrive and pass through. Following the reserve battalion of the assaulting brigade would come the remainder of 1st Special Service Brigade in the shape of 3 and 6 Commandos and 45 Royal Marine Commando. Their task was to move straight off the landing beach and advance to link up with and reinforce 6th Airborne Division on the eastern side of the River Orne.

All of these landings were programmed to be completed at H Hour (the time the first waves were due to touch down) plus 120 minutes. Then came the intermediate brigade, 185th Brigade, comprising 2nd Warwickshires, 1st Royal Norfolks and 2nd King's Shropshire Light Infantry. All three battalions would strike out for the vital D-Day objective of Caen with all speed, supported by the tanks of 27th Armoured Brigade. The reserve brigade, 9th Brigade, was to begin its landings at H Hour + 270 minutes. Its three battalions (2nd Lincolnshires, 1st King's Own Scottish Borderers and 2nd Royal Ulster Rifles), supported by tanks, would drive on Caen along the right flank of the beachhead as soon as they cleared the waterfront.

THE LANDINGS: THE AIRBORNE ASSAULT

LEFT **The original Caen Canal lifting-bridge captured by Maj Howard and his company during the first minutes of D-Day. It now lies in the grounds of the Airborne Museum at Bénouville, moved there after it was replaced by a more modern structure. (Ken Ford)**

OPPOSITE TOP **Major-General Richard Gale is given a present of a tin of treacle by the RAF station commander, Group Captain Surplice, as he boards glider number 70 ready for his passage to Normandy to join the main body of 6th Airborne Division. (Imperial War Museum, H39072)**

OPPOSITE BOTTOM **The bridge over the River Orne at Bénouville. This was the second target of Maj John Howard's D Company of the 2nd Oxfordshire and Buckinghamshire Light Infantry, and it was captured intact in the early minutes of 6 June. Its fame and place in history has been long overshadowed by the more glamorous events at Pegasus Bridge over the Caen Canal a few hundred yards away. (Imperial War Museum, B5230)**

OVERLEAF **PEGASUS BRIDGE Lt Den Brotheridge leads No 1 Platoon into the attack across the canal bridge at Bénouville. With the gliders landing so close to their objective the paratroopers of the Ox and Bucks Light Infantry were able to get onto the bridge virtually undetected. Close behind Brotheridge was Private Billy Gray, carrying a Bren gun. The two German guards patrolling the bridge were suddenly confronted by the paras rushing towards**

A s darkness was falling at 2256hrs on 5 June 1944, six Horsa gliders were pulled airborne from the runway at Tarrant Rushton airfield in England by six Halifax bombers. Inside the wood and canvas gliders were troops from D Company of 2nd Oxfordshire and Buckinghamshire Light Infantry, part of 6th Airlanding Brigade of British 6th Airborne Division. The troops were commanded by Major John Howard and were the *coup de main* party ordered to attack the bridges over the Orne river and Caen canal at Bénouville in Normandy. Seven minutes later, 70 miles away to the north-east, more planes from No. 38 Group RAF lifted into the sky from Harwell airfield in Berkshire. This time, Albemarle aircraft carried the men of 22nd Independent Parachute Company, whose task was to drop onto and mark out landing zones ready for the main parachute force who were set to arrive 30 minutes after them. The airborne invasion of Hitler's Fortress Europe was at last under way.

THE CAPTURE OF THE ORNE BRIDGES

At 0007hrs (British Double Summer Time) on 6 June, Sergeant Jim Wallwork cast off his glider from the tug aircraft and began the descent to his designated landing zone (LZ 'X') close by the Orne bridges. Behind him, following at one minute intervals, came the other five Horsas carrying the remainder of Maj Howard's small force. At 0016hrs them out of the night. Private Romer turned and fled but the other managed to fire off a red flare to raise the alarm. Brotheridge reacted immediately and cut the man down with a burst of Sten gun fire; Billy Gray then joined in with a volley from his Bren gun, The firing alerted the machine gun crew on the end of the bridge. Brotheridge continued towards them tossing a grenade as he ran, but was instantly killed by a bullet through the neck. Following closely behind Brotheridge, the men of his platoon concentrated their fire on the German machine gun post. The grenade thrown by the now dead officer exploded killing the enemy gun crew. Without pause, the men of the platoon continued their race across the bridge and fanned out on the other side of the canal. In just a few swift seconds the first Allied objective had been captured. The first Allied soldier had been killed in action on D-Day and the first German soldier had died defending Hitler's Fortress Europe. The war continued for the other men on the bridge. Within minutes Private Romer, a 16-year old Berliner fresh from training camp, was captured. For Billy Gray and his comrades in 'D' Company, the fighting was only just beginning. After the capture of the bridge the company joined the remainder of the 2nd Oxs and Bucks and went into the line as infantry early on 7 June. For the next seven weeks they fought an increasingly bitter war of attrition to protect the left flank of the landings. Little by little the battalion's strength was eroded by artillery, machine guns and snipers. By the end of August Major Howard's 'D' Company was a shadow of its former strength. All of the original sergeants and most of the corporals were gone, and of the officers on D-Day only Howard was left, and he had been wounded twice. Altogether, the company could only muster 40 of the 181 men who began the campaign.

(Howard Gerrard)

Wallwork brought his aircraft to a grinding halt just 60yds from the bridge over the Orne Canal. Howard and his men quickly crashed their way out of the aircraft's flimsy structure and dashed for the bridge. In the lead was Lieutenant Den Brotheridge. He led his men through the barbed wire surrounding the bridge and onto the roadway. Behind them, almost silently, the next two gliders swept in and landed just a few yards from Wallwork's plane. The skill of three glider pilots, Sergeants Wallwork, Boland and Hobbs, had delivered almost 90 men across the Channel to within 100yds of their objective.

Howard's men now set about the tasks for which they had spent so many months training. The operation worked like clockwork.

Lieutenant Brotheridge and No. 1 Platoon were swiftly onto the road and they began running across the bridge to get among the enemy weapons pits on the far side of the structure. On the bridge, striding aimlessly back and forth, were two German sentries. They had not heard the arrival of the gliders above the noise of aircraft and anti-aircraft fire and were suddenly startled to see the blackened faces of British troops rushing towards them. One sentry turned and ran whilst the other managed to get off a flare to raise the alarm. Almost immediately he was killed by a burst of Sten gunfire from Brotheridge. Next, the lieutenant rushed towards the machine gun, which was positioned in a sandbagged pit at the end of the bridge, throwing a grenade as he went. The now awakened MG42 crew saw him coming and opened fire on the young officer, killing him instantly. However, the gun was quickly silenced by the troops following behind Brotheridge.

By now the German defenders were fully roused and fighting back. No. 1 Platoon began clearing the enemy from the western side of the canal around the bridge, throwing grenades and firing as they went. On the eastern side of the lifting-bridge, Lieutenant Wood and his No. 2 Platoon broke free from the second glider and cleared the German trenches, machine gun positions and a 50mm anti-tank gun on that side of the canal. The third glider contained No. 3 Platoon commanded by Lt Smith, and had a bumpy landing. Six of the platoon remained trapped in the glider when the lieutenant and the others leapt from the aircraft to join up with Howard. The major directed Smith to take his men over the bridge and help No. 1 Platoon to clear the western canal bank and form a defensive perimeter. As this was happening, sappers began checking the underside of the bridge for demolition charges, cutting any wires that they came across, but they found no explosives in position. (It later transpired that the charges allocated for the bridge were stored in a hut nearby and were only to be put in place when directed by higher authority). The enemy had been caught entirely unprepared for the assault.

Meanwhile, a few hundred yards to the east, Howard's other three platoons were dropping in their gliders towards the bridge over the

River Orne. Unfortunately, the leading glider carrying Howard's second in command, Captain Priday, had been cast adrift in the wrong place and landed near the River Dives five miles away. The other two, however, made a successful landing within a few hundred yards of their objective and the river bridge was captured with little opposition.

The initial operation had been a complete success. Within just 15 minutes both bridges had been captured and made secure with a minimum of casualties. When Howard received news of the capture of the river bridge, he ordered the success signal 'Ham and Jam' to be transmitted to signify that he had the intact bridges under his control. It now only remained for him and his company to hold them until they were relieved by the paratroopers of Lieutenant-Colonel Pine Coffin's 7th Parachute Battalion, who were to land on DZ 'N' 30 minutes later.

The pathfinders of the 22nd Independent Parachute Company, who had leapt into Normandy just a few minutes after Maj Howard's company had descended on the bridges, did not have such a successful landing. Their drops were scattered and it took a long time for the men to rally. Two aircraft had been allocated to deliver men to each of the three drop zones. They were then to set up their Eureka beacons to guide in the main force of paratroopers onto their allocated landing points. This main force was arranged to drop 30 minutes after the pathfinders. The 5th Parachute Brigade's Commander, Brigadier Nigel Poett, arrived with his advance HQ precisely on target on DZ 'N', close by Ranville with the pathfinders. He was immediately cheered by the sound of the whistle being blown by Maj Howard, signalling the successful capture of the bridges.

With so little time to complete their tasks and the failure of the majority of them to land on target, the pathfinders were unable to mark the drop zones sufficiently well to ensure that the following paratroopers landed in the correct place. When the aircraft bringing the main force arrived over their various drop zones at around 0045hrs, the beacons guiding them onto their targets were giving misleading signals. German anti-aircraft fire was also causing many planes to lose formation and direction, so when the order came for the parachutists to drop, they were often released in the wrong places.

On DZ 'N', 5th Parachute Brigade was dispersed over a wide area. The 7th, 12th and 13th Parachute Battalions became intermingled and confused. Some order was restored as the individual groups quickly assembled at their appropriate collecting points, but many paratroopers became completely lost and only joined up with their units after many hours or even days trying to get their bearings.

Lieutenant-Colonel Pine Coffin's 7th Parachute Battalion dropped on the Ranville DZ 'N' in some disarray. After waiting at the rendezvous point for a short while for his battalion to rally, the colonel decided to take those men who had arrived and lead them towards Howard's

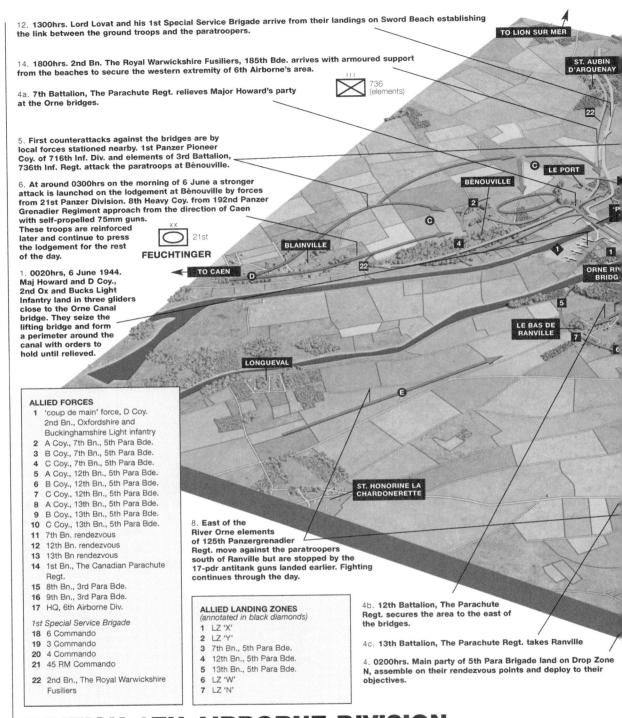

12. **1300hrs.** Lord Lovat and his 1st Special Service Brigade arrive from their landings on Sword Beach establishing the link between the ground troops and the paratroopers.

14. **1800hrs.** 2nd Bn. The Royal Warwickshire Fusiliers, 185th Bde. arrives with armoured support from the beaches to secure the western extremity of 6th Airborne's area.

4a. **7th Battalion, The Parachute Regt.** relieves Major Howard's party at the Orne bridges.

5. First counterattacks against the bridges are by local forces stationed nearby. 1st Panzer Pioneer Coy. of 716th Inf. Div. and elements of 3rd Battalion, 736th Inf. Regt. attack the paratroops at Bènouville.

6. At around 0300hrs on the morning of 6 June a stronger attack is launched on the lodgement at Bènouville by forces from 21st Panzer Division. 8th Heavy Coy. from 192nd Panzer Grenadier Regiment approach from the direction of Caen with self-propelled 75mm guns. These troops are reinforced later and continue to press the lodgement for the rest of the day.

FEUCHTINGER 21st

1. **0020hrs, 6 June 1944.** Maj Howard and D Coy., 2nd Ox and Bucks Light Infantry land in three gliders close to the Orne Canal bridge. They seize the lifting bridge and form a perimeter around the canal with orders to hold until relieved.

736 (elements)

TO LION SUR MER
ST. AUBIN D'ARQUENAY
22
LE PORT
BÈNOUVILLE
C
2
C
4
BLAINVILLE
TO CAEN
22
ORNE RIVER BRIDGE
LE BAS DE RANVILLE
5
7
LONGUEVAL
E
ST. HONORINE LA CHARDONERETTE

ALLIED FORCES
1 'coup de main' force, D Coy. 2nd Bn., Oxfordshire and Buckinghamshire Light infantry
2 A Coy., 7th Bn., 5th Para Bde.
3 B Coy., 7th Bn., 5th Para Bde.
4 C Coy., 7th Bn., 5th Para Bde.
5 A Coy., 12th Bn., 5th Para Bde.
6 B Coy., 12th Bn., 5th Para Bde.
7 C Coy., 12th Bn., 5th Para Bde.
8 A Coy., 13th Bn., 5th Para Bde.
9 B Coy., 13th Bn., 5th Para Bde.
10 C Coy., 13th Bn., 5th Para Bde.
11 7th Bn. rendezvous
12 12th Bn. rendezvous
13 13th Bn rendezvous
14 1st Bn., The Canadian Parachute Regt.
15 8th Bn., 3rd Para Bde.
16 9th Bn., 3rd Para Bde.
17 HQ, 6th Airborne Div.

1st Special Service Brigade
18 6 Commando
19 3 Commando
20 4 Commando
21 45 RM Commando

22 2nd Bn., The Royal Warwickshire Fusiliers

8. East of the River Orne elements of 125th Panzergrenadier Regt. move against the paratroopers south of Ranville but are stopped by the 17-pdr antitank guns landed earlier. Fighting continues through the day.

ALLIED LANDING ZONES
(annotated in black diamonds)
1 LZ 'X'
2 LZ 'Y'
3 7th Bn., 5th Para Bde.
4 12th Bn., 5th Para Bde.
5 13th Bn., 5th Para Bde.
6 LZ 'W'
7 LZ 'N'

4b. **12th Battalion, The Parachute Regt.** secures the area to the east of the bridges.

4c. **13th Battalion, The Parachute Regt.** takes Ranville.

4. **0200hrs.** Main party of 5th Para Brigade land on Drop Zone N, assemble on their rendezvous points and deploy to their objectives.

BRITISH 6TH AIRBORNE DIVISION – THE EASTERN FLANK

6 June 1944, 0020hrs–2100hrs, viewed from the southeast showing the parachute and glider assault by British 6th Airborne Division. This included the capture of the two vital bridges near Bènouville across the Orne River and the Caen Canal – 'Pegasus' Bridge. Also shown are the increasingly powerful German counterattacks as the defenders respond to the Allied attack.

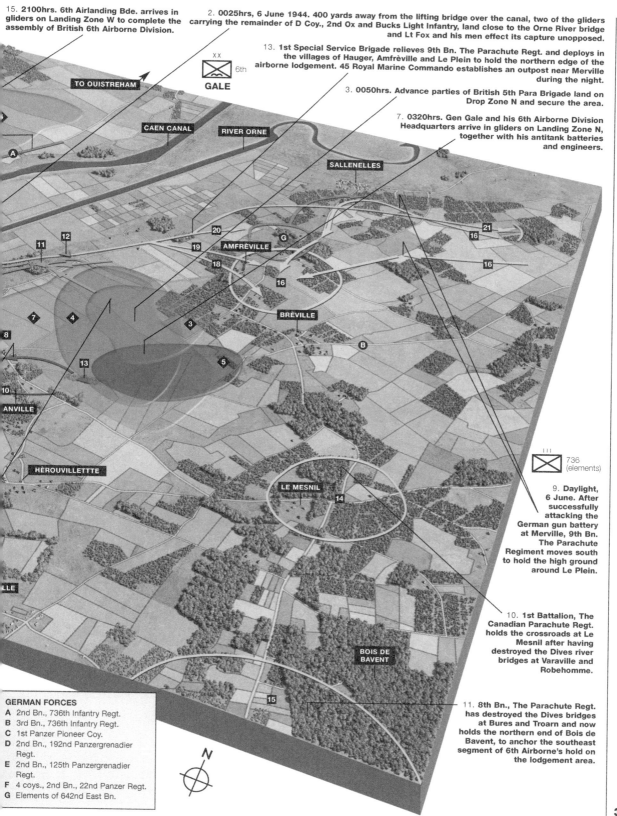

15. **2100hrs. 6th Airlanding Bde. arrives in gliders on Landing Zone W to complete the assembly of British 6th Airborne Division.**

2. **0025hrs, 6 June 1944. 400 yards away from the lifting bridge over the canal, two of the gliders carrying the remainder of D Coy., 2nd Ox and Bucks Light Infantry, land close to the Orne River bridge and Lt Fox and his men effect its capture unopposed.**

13. **1st Special Service Brigade relieves 9th Bn. The Parachute Regt. and deploys in the villages of Hauger, Amfréville and Le Plein to hold the northern edge of the airborne lodgement. 45 Royal Marine Commando establishes an outpost near Merville during the night.**

3. **0050hrs. Advance parties of British 5th Para Brigade land on Drop Zone N and secure the area.**

7. **0320hrs. Gen Gale and his 6th Airborne Division Headquarters arrive in gliders on Landing Zone N, together with his antitank batteries and engineers.**

TO OUISTREHAM

XX
6th
GALE

CAEN CANAL

RIVER ORNE

SALLENELLES

A

20

19

AMFRÉVILLE

18

G

16

21

16

16

11

12

7

4

8

13

3

BRÉVILLE

B

5

10

ANVILLE

HÉROUVILLETTTE

LE MESNIL

14

III
736
(elements)

9. **Daylight, 6 June. After successfully attacking the German gun battery at Merville, 9th Bn. The Parachute Regiment moves south to hold the high ground around Le Plein.**

10. **1st Battalion, The Canadian Parachute Regt. holds the crossroads at Le Mesnil after having destroyed the Dives river bridges at Varaville and Robehomme.**

BOIS DE BAVENT

15

11. **8th Bn., The Parachute Regt. has destroyed the Dives bridges at Bures and Troarn and now holds the northern end of Bois de Bavent, to anchor the southeast segment of 6th Airborne's hold on the lodgement area.**

LLE

N

GERMAN FORCES
A 2nd Bn., 736th Infantry Regt.
B 3rd Bn., 736th Infantry Regt.
C 1st Panzer Pioneer Coy.
D 2nd Bn., 192nd Panzergrenadier Regt.
E 2nd Bn., 125th Panzergrenadier Regt.
F 4 coys, 2nd Bn., 22nd Panzer Regt.
G Elements of 642nd East Bn.

isolated company of the Ox and Bucks at the Orne bridges. He left his second in command, Major Baume, to collect any stragglers who might turn up later. The battalion's arrival at the bridges was most opportune, as the enemy was beginning to launch determined counter-attacks against howard's exposed company. Pine Coffin now took over command of the bridges and organised a strong perimeter around the river and canal crossings. Howard's company was withdrawn to the eastern river bridge to act as reserve, whilst the 7th Battalion's own companies crossed over the Caen Canal and established defensive positions on the western side of the lodgement. A and C Companies blocked the road from Caen, holding the southern part of the village of Bénouville, whilst B Company moved into place in the tiny hamlet of Le Port and in the small wood alongside it, blocking the approaches from Ouistreham. The battalion was only 200 strong, although other paratroopers filtered in during the night as isolated individuals picked their way through the darkness to join their unit.

Private Frank Gardner, Captain Brian Priday and Lance-Corpora B. Lambley of D Company, 2nd Oxfordshire and Buckinghamshire Light Infantry. These men were part of the *cou de main* party designated to capture the river bridge over the Orne at Bénouville, but their glider landed ten miles away from their objective close to the River Dives. It took several days for them to find their way through enemy territory to join up with their battalion. (Imperial War Museum, B5586)

THE CAPTURE OF THE MERVILLE BATTERY

The 5th Parachute Brigade's other two battalions also had a scattered drop around DZ 'N'. Its 12th Battalion, commanded by Lieutenant-Colonel Johnny Johnson, planned to rendezvous in a quarry alongside the Ranville-Sallenelles road, but the dispersed nature of the drop had meant that many of its men had come down in the woods and orchards to the east of the zone. After almost an hour only 60 per cent of the unit's strength had arrived at the rallying point. Lieutenant-Colonel Johnson decided that he had enough strength to move and led his men to their appointed task of defending the south-western point of the landings around Le Bas de Ranville. The 13th Parachute Battalion, commanded by Lieutenant-Colonel Luard, was also dispersed over a large area. Nonetheless, within an hour Luard had gathered around 60 per cent of his men and advanced from the rendezvous point to capture the important village of Ranville.

To the north-east, on DZ 'V', Gale's 3rd Parachute Brigade, commanded by Brigadier James Hill, also experienced a somewhat disorganised arrival in Normandy. The brigade's two battalions – 9th Parachute Battalion and 1st Canadian Parachute Battalion – were scattered across woods, fields and flooded valleys all around the drop zone. Lieutenant-Colonel Terence Otway's men of the 9th Parachute Battalion, tasked with attacking the Merville Battery, were the most dispersed of all.

The gun battery at Merville overlooking Sword Beach was a very important target. Its field of fire dominated the sea lane into

Ouistreham, through which the invasion ships would have to pass. The 9th Parachute Battalion had to eliminate the battery before 0500hrs or the cruiser HMS *Arethusa* would attempt to destroy the position with its guns. The battery's weapons were enclosed in an area 700 x 500yds, surrounded by a double belt of barbed wire 15ft thick and 5ft high, with minefields dotted between them. The guns themselves were housed in steel-doored concrete emplacements 6ft thick, two of which were covered with 12ft of earth. An anti-tank ditch barred approach from the seaward side and a total of 15 weapons pits protected all approaches. In addition to the 750 men of the battalion engaged in the operation, Otway was equipped with heavy mortars, an anti-tank gun, jeeps with trailers full of demolition stores and flame-throwers, all of which were carried to the landing zone in five Horsa gliders. It was planned that, at the time of the assault, three gliders would land a further 50 men directly onto the roofs of the guns within the battery itself.

The aircraft carrying the battalion had found it difficult to identify the drop zone through the haze and smoke caused by an RAF bombing raid on the Merville Battery shortly before their arrival. Many of Otway's men were dropped to the east of DZ 'V' in the marshes of the River Dives, some as far away as the high ground between Cabourg and Dozule. The colonel knew that time was of the essence, for the battery had to be eliminated before the ships of the invasion fleet came within range of the guns. Impatiently he waited for his force to gather, with men appearing out of the night in ones and twos, each cautiously moving through the darkness, evading scattered German infantry as they moved toward the battalion's rendezvous point.

By 0300hrs Otway knew that he would have to go with the men he had if he was to stand any chance of capturing the battery before daylight. He had only 150 of the 750 paratroopers of his battalion with which to carry out the attack. None of the five gliders carrying the jeeps, trailers and anti-tank guns allocated to the battalion had appeared, nor had the 3in. mortars, demolition engineers, medical teams or naval bombardment parties. Nonetheless, Otway and his small party set out for Merville, determined to execute the important task that had been set

The rear of Merville Battery's Casemate 1, the largest of the four gun positions. To the right is a doorway leading up steps to a 'tobruk' weapons pit on the roof. Covering the main door is a machine-gun embrasure. (Ken Ford)

The front of the Merville Battery's Casemate Number 1 facing out towards Sword Beach on the far side of the River Orne. It housed a fairly modest 75mm gun rather than the much larger 150mm calibre coast gun that was expected by Allied planners. (Ken Ford)

them. When LtCol Otway arrived in the vicinity of the battery he was met by Major George Smith and his party, who had landed earlier to reconnoitre the site. Major Smith told him that the bombing raid had caused very little damage and had mostly missed the objective. Smith did, however, have some good news for Otway, for he and two warrant officers had cut their way through the outer wire of the German strongpoint, passed through the minefield and arrived at the inner wire where they observed enemy posts and located German positions, all without arousing the attention of the battery's garrison. A taping party led by Captain Paul Greenway, had also successfully cleared and marked four routes through the minefield even though they had no mine detectors or marking tape.

With only 20 per cent of his force and no heavy weapons, mine detectors or mortars, LtCol Otway was determined that the attack should still go in, timed to coincide with the arrival of the three gliders directly onto the guns. He was hoping that confusion caused by the two-pronged assault would divert the enemy's attention and hamper an effective reaction. There were not enough men to make the attack through the four paths created through the minefield, so only two of the lanes were used, with one party to go in through the wire and attack the casemates whilst the remainder of Otway's group attacked the main gate. As the men were preparing to rush the battery, a German machine gun post spotted the movement and opened fire, alerting the enemy garrison. At the same time the sound of aircraft overhead signalled the arrival of the gliders. Otway ordered the attack to start immediately and the fire fight for the possession of the battery began.

Two of the gliders now swooped down towards the fortified area; the third had got into trouble after take-off and had returned to base. Winding up to meet them came the snaking trails of tracer fire as the German defenders brought anti-aircraft weapons to bear on the gliders. Both aircraft were hit repeatedly, with the small cannon shells ripping through the canvas and wood sides of the planes and starting small fires which were fanned by the slipstream. Otway was unable to illuminate the ttery with flares because he had no mortars with which to fire his star ells. Disorientated by the fire and darkness, the gliders both missed e target. One landed 200yds from the perimeter, whilst the other came own two miles away. Neither group was able to play any role in the sault.

Otway's men pressed through the gaps in the outer wire and onto the ntanglements protecting the inner zone. Bangalore torpedoes (metal pes filled with explosives) blasted a way through this second band and moments the paratroopers were amongst the gun emplacements. In e darkness it was difficult to identify friend from foe. The paratroopers ceived fire from all sides and all angles. One by one the trenches and eapons pits scattered around the site were cleared in hand-to-hand ghting, as the enemy infantry put up spirited resistance. However, their solve quickly began to crumble when they realised they were being tacked by paratroopers. Up went the cry *Fallschirmjäger!*, and the sistance began to melt away. The conscripted foreigners and old men of e 716th Division had no wish to tangle with elite forces in the dark – the utcome could be only certain death. The garrison surrendered. With me running out for Otway and his men before the naval ombardment was due to crash into the battery, demolition teams quickly ent amongst the guns, placing charges in their breaches and spiking ch piece. Otway's men were disappointed to discover the guns were latively small 75mm field guns and not the 150mm coastal guns the aratroopers had expected to find, but the main thing was that the battery ad been eliminated as ordered. The job done, Otway rallied his men and ithdrew the remnants of his battalion towards the high ground near Le lein as planned, just as German artillery fire began to pound the area. Of e 150 men who started the assault, only about 80 remained on their feet.

HE DESTRUCTION OF BRIDGES
VER THE RIVER DIVES

ropping with the 9th Parachute Battalion on 3rd Parachute Brigade's Z 'V' was the 1st Canadian Parachute Battalion, commanded by ieutenant-Colonel George Bradbrooke. The Canadians were ordered to low the bridges over the River Dives at Varaville and Robehomme nd to eliminate the German garrison at Varaville. As with the other attalions, its drop was scattered and disorganised. Many of C Company's ien were dropped ten miles from the correct zone, some even coming own within 1,000yds of the landing beaches on the western side of the iver Orne. A few, however, were dropped close enough to the drop zone form an assault group to attack the German garrison in Varaville. hese men, under the command of Major McLeod, were joined by ragglers from A Company and others from 8th and 9th Parachute attalions. It took most of the night for this small band to eliminate ie Germans in Varaville, who were mainly grouped around a fortified osition near the chateau. Whilst the Canadians were engaging the arrison they heard an enormous roar as the bridge over the Dives near he village was blown. A small group of men under Sergeant Davies had ianaged to assemble enough explosives and had infiltrated through the nemy positions to set about destroying the crossing place as planned.

B Company lost many of its men in the flooded waters and marshy ground of the River Dives. Its objective was the bridge at Robehomme. Only a few paratroopers could be gathered together for the task and these men set off for the river led by Lieutenant Toseland. At the crossing place they found Major Fuller, who had earlier dropped in the River Dives itself. The engineers tasked with the blowing of the bridge had not arrived, nor had their explosives. Each man did, however, have a small amount of explosive with him to make Gammon bombs to be used against tanks, and so the major gathered all of the explosives together to form a single charge of about 30lbs. One of the sergeants used this charge to try to blow the bridge, but only succeeded in weakening it. Fortunately, some time later a group of engineers arrived and placed adequate charges on the structure, destroying it completely. With both of these bridges blown, the 1st Canadian Battalion withdrew to the area of Le Mesnil to take up a position guarding the eastern flank of the airborne lodgement.

Further to the south, 3rd Parachute Brigade's other battalion, the 8th Parachute Battalion, under the command of Lieutenant-Colonel Alastair Pearson, dropped onto DZ 'K'. It had the most scattered drop of all, for only four of the 37 C47s carrying the battalion dropped their sticks of paras at the right place. Two hundred and thirty men were dropped on DZ 'N' instead of DZ 'K'. The battalion's task was the elimination of the bridges over the Dives at Bures and Troarn. Lieutenant-Colonel Pearson found the same chaos as elsewhere when he had landed and tried to gather his battalion together. At the rendezvous near a track junction close to Touffreville he could only find 30 of his men. The colonel waited for more to arrive and by 0330hrs he had assembled 11 officers and 130 other ranks. Time was pressing and he could wait no longer; he decided that this depleted force would have to do, and set about achieving his objectives. He sent a small party off to destroy the railway bridge at Bures and took the remainder of his men towards Troarn. This latter village was the greater problem, for it was thought to be held in force by the enemy and the bridge was on the far side of the built-up area.

This Horsa glider is alleged to be the one that carried MajGen Gal over to Normandy, but it lacks the number 70 that was marked on the fuselage to the right of the door and which can clearly be seen in other photographs of the general emplaning for the flight. (Imperial War Museum, B5600)

Lieutenant-Colonel Pearson gathered a few more men as he advanced, and deployed what he had of his battalion to command the high ground overlooking Troarn. Meanwhile, other men of his unit and some engineers had been gathering near DZ 'N', where they had been dropped by mistake. They consisted of two separate parties who had met up near the Bavent Woods. The senior officer was Major J. Roseveare, a Royal Engineer from 3rd Parachute Squadron RE. The combined party consisted of about 60 paratroopers and 60 engineers, together with 400lbs of explosives, demolition equipment and a jeep and trailer. The major sent the bulk of the engineers and most of the material to blow the Bures bridge, whilst he and eight others loaded the trailer with as much explosive as they could, piled onto the jeep and headed for Troarn.

Just outside the village they found a barbed wire roadblock, which took 20 minutes to negotiate. Whilst they were doing so, one of the men shot a German cyclist, rousing the enemy garrison. The whole area came alive with Germans, and the intrepid party once more crammed onto the jeep and trailer and set off down the main street firing as they went. 'There seemed to be a Boche in every doorway shooting like mad,' recalled Maj Roseveare later. The engineers returned fire as best they could whilst clinging desperately to the swaying vehicle as it careered at speed down the street. Nobody was injured, but the sapper on the rear of the trailer, who had been firing a Bren gun, was missing when they reached the unguarded road bridge. Working as quickly as they could, they laid explosives and blew the charges. When the dust settled, there was a large impassable gap in the middle of the roadway. Job completed, the major and his men abandoned the jeep and made their way on foot back to the battalion's lines, swimming small streams and fording inundated areas as they went.

It was later that morning before LtCol Pearson received confirmation that both the bridges at Troarn and Bures had been demolished as

This picture was taken on 10 June, four days after the landings. It shows a group of paratroopers from 12th Parachute Battalion who were dropped in enemy territory far from DZ 'N' and spent the next four days trying to link up with their battalion. They now enjoy a deserved cup of tea. (Imperial War Museum, B5349)

ordered, although he had heard the tremendous explosions earlier. His battalion was strengthened during the night as more stragglers rejoined the unit. By dawn, the colonel had his men deployed along the ridge down the western side of the Bavent Wood and was overlooking the enemy-held territory to the east.

Whilst the individual battalions of the first two brigades of the 6th Airborne Division were completing their assigned tasks, MajGen Gale and his headquarters had arrived with the third wave of the division, landing on DZ 'N' at around 0320hrs. The general had set down with the main glider force, and with him were the heavy equipment, light field-guns and anti-tank guns that had been carried over to Normandy in 68 Horsa and four giant Hamilcar gliders. The arrival of Gale and his headquarters now meant that the paratroopers could fight as a division, rather than as a collection of separate battalions each fighting their own individual war.

Just after dawn, information began to filter through to Gale at his HQ. News of the capture of the bridges over the Orne and Caen Canal, the destruction of the Merville Battery and the blowing of all the bridges over the Dives gave the general great heart. His division had achieved all their major objectives; it now remained for his specialist paras to fight as infantry and to hold on to the lodgement against the inevitable German counter-attacks.

GERMAN REACTION TO THE AIRBORNE LANDINGS

Generalleutnant Wilhelm Richter, commander of the German 716th Infantry Division, received news of the Allied airborne landings at around 0120hrs. He learned that some of his units were in action against British paratroops in several places east of the River Orne. He also heard that the Orne bridges at Bénouville had been captured intact. He quickly contacted the commander of 21st Panzer Division, Generalmajor Edgar Feuchtinger, at his headquarters at St Pierre sur Dives and ordered him to get his nearest units to attack the landings. By 0200hrs, the large scale of the Allied operations became apparent and it was clear that it would take a major counter-attack to deal with them. Richter asked Feuchtinger to bring forward the whole of his armoured division to clear the area east of the Orne of British paratroopers.

Feuchtinger hesitated: whilst it was true that his division came under the 716th Division as a result of the attack made against that division, he was also aware that the 21st Panzers were a component part of the German High Command's (OKW) armoured reserve. To support the coast defence division with localised units was one thing, but to release the whole of his armoured division against what might still prove to be a diversionary raid, was something more serious and would have to be confirmed by a higher authority. This approval was very slow in coming, for all the way up and down the chain of command from Feuchtinger to OKW, delay and indecision seemed to dominate. Nobody could agree if the situation warranted the release of the armoured reserves. Were the British paratroopers part of an invasion or just a diversion? It took almost 12 hours before anyone could decide. In the meantime, those troops in the area of the landings would have to deal with the invaders unaided.

Closer to the Orne, way down the chain of command, other German officers were reacting more positively. The men of Richter's 736th Regiment had units in action to counter the landings that were taking place amongst them. The British had also descended close to villages where some of Feuchtinger's Panzer units were garrisoned. These units were in contact with the British not because they had been ordered into action, but because the British paratroopers had landed virtually on top of them.

In the southern part of the landing zones, east of the Orne, companies from III Battalion, 125th Panzergrenadiers, part of 21st Panzer Division, were grouped around Troarn, Sannerville and Colombelles. These units went into action immediately. In the north, especially near Bavent and Sallenelles, were companies of the 642nd East Battalion, who were attached to 736th Infantry Regiment, and these companies formed the bulk of the troops countering the landing on LZ 'V'. At Merville and on the coast at Franceville-Plage, a company from III Battalion, 736th Regiment and one from the 642nd East Battalion found themselves responding to the attack of LtCol Otway and his 9th Battalion.

All of these German units were in the area at the time of the airborne landings, and they were simply reacting to an enemy who had landed among them. The first counter-attack by units outside the area came from a hastily assembled force put together under Gen Richter's orders. He knew that the main objective of such a counter-attack had to be the recapture of the Benouville bridges. The closest units on the western side of the Orne were elements of Feuchtinger's II Battalion 192nd Panzergrenadiers at Cairon. This battalion moved off towards Bénouville just after 0200hrs under the command of Major Zippe, who was ordered to retake the bridges, cross over the Orne and attack the British from the west. To assist it, from the north, Richter sent his 1st Panzerjäger Company together with guns from the 989th Heavy Artillery Battalion.

The first of Maj Zippe's units into action was the 8th Heavy Company under Leutnant Braats, with its three self-propelled 75mm guns, a 20mm flak troop on armoured carriers and a troop of mortars. They attacked down the road from Caen at around 0330hrs and met Pine Coffin's two companies on the outskirts of Benouville. The paratroopers defended doggedly, blunting the attack. A and C Companies of the 7th Parachute Battalion were forced back into Benouville in the process, but their perimeter held. The Germans were incapable of penetrating this defensive ring without armour. The Panzer grenadiers therefore dug themselves in and spent the remainder of the night making localised assaults and pounding the area with machine gun and mortar fire, waiting for the tanks to arrive. Occasional sorties made against the paratroopers' lines came close to a breakthrough, but the 7th Battalion was determined that it would not be moved. Through the night and

This picture was labelled: 'troops looking for Allied paratroopers,' and probably shows men from German 716th Division trying to locate scattered individuals from Gen Gale's British 6th Airborne Division near the River Dives. (Bundesarchiv, 96/49/25A)

throughout most of the following day, Pine Coffin's men held on to t'
vital bridgehead on the eastern side of the Orne.

The Panzergrenadiers of Feuchtinger's division also attacked on t
eastern side of the Orne. Those units of 125th Panzergrenad
Regiment who were close to the landings were engaged in the mid
of the night, but the main counter-attack came later in the mornir
The 12th and 13th Parachute Battalions, who were holding the sou
western flank of the lodgement from the River Orne to Herouville
were attacked by German infantry and self-propelled guns from bo
battalions of the 125th Panzergrenadiers. The British had very go
defensive positions on a reverse slope, well concealed from the ener
with about 1,000yds of open ground in front, forcing any German atta
to cross the crest and expose itself to the waiting paras below.

Successive counter-attacks were beaten off by the paratroopers, usin
their six 6-pdr. and three 17-pdr. anti-tank guns, together with some
the division's light artillery. Although this fighting around Ranville a
Herouvillete was often fierce and the enemy did force his way clo
to the British lines, Gen Gale was never seriously worried about t
situation in this sector.

With the dawn of D-Day and with landing-craft closing inexorably
the invasion beaches, Gen Gale could feel pleased with the performan
of his division. The southern flank was secured by Poett's 12th and 13
Battalions; LtCol Pearson's 8th Battalion was ensconced on the ridg
within Bavent Wood; the 1st Canadian Parachute Battalion held th
eastern stop line through Le Mesnil; Otway's 9th Battalion held the hig
ground around Le Plein; and LtCol Pine Coffin's 7th Battalion held th
perimeter around the Caen Canal bridges through Benouville and I
Port. Although this last sector was the most precarious, the situatic
was difficult but not critical. It now remained for MajGen Gale and h
paratroopers to hold out until the troops landing on Sword Beach cam
to their relief.

A Mitchell medium bomber,
complete with Allied recognition
stripes, returning from a raid on
the invasion coast, passes over a
convoy on its way to France.
(Imperial War Museum, CL106)

THE LANDINGS: SWORD BEACH

Early in the morning of 6 June 1944, at around 0300hrs, Allied air forces began the final aerial bombardment of Hitler's Atlantic Wall defences and artillery sites along the invasion beaches. Strongpoints close to the shoreline of Sword Beach and fortified areas in the rear were also located and attacked. This softening-up process resumed a few hours later when naval Force S arrived seven miles offshore and began its bombardment of the same areas. HMS *Warspite* and *Ramillies*, together with the monitor *Roberts* pounded the German long-range gun batteries at Villerville, Benerville and Houlgate with their 15in. weapons, whilst the cruisers *Scylla*, *Danae*, *Dragon*, *Frobisher*, *Arethusa* and *Mauritius* attacked the shore batteries and strongpoints around Sword. In return, the enemy replied in a desultory manner with few of their shots falling anywhere near the naval ships. A little later, when daylight allowed the fall of shot to be observed, the smaller destroyers moved in close to shore to add their weight of fire to the bombardment.

At about 0510hrs, low-flying aircraft from the RAF laid a smoke screen to the east of Force S to help shield its ships from the long-range enemy guns at Le Havre. Unfortunately, torpedo boats from the German 5th Torpedo Boat Flotilla took advantage of this screen to approach the bombarding ships and loosed off a total of 15 torpedoes at the Allied vessels. Most of their torpedoes missed, but the German boats did have one success, with the Norwegian destroyer *Svenner* taking a hit on her port beam immediately under her boiler room. The vessel broke in two but, despite sinking rapidly, most of her crew were saved.

To the starboard of this bombardment fleet, a great convoy of transport shipping arrived at their designated lowering positions and hove to. At 0530hrs soldiers clambered on to the decks of these transport ships and began the long, slow process of boarding the light Landing Craft Assault (LCA) that would take them to the shores of Normandy. On board the LSIs (Landing Ship Infantry) *Glenearn* and *Cutlass*, the assault companies of 1st South Lancs and 2nd East Yorks clambered down the nets and onto the bobbing craft. At about the same time, eight LCTs (Landing Craft Tank) moved slowly away from the lowering point towards the shore, carrying the DD tanks of the 13th/18th Hussars.

The Run-in to the Beaches

At 0600hrs, with the rising sun still obscured by an overcast sky, the LCAs left their mother ship and set out for Queen Red and Queen White Beaches, along with ten LCTs carrying the assault groups of specialised armour from 79th Division. Fourteen minutes later, flanking the assault force, five LCT(R)s (Landing Craft Rocket) left the lowering position for their run-in to the beaches. Another nine minutes and a further 19 LCTs, containing the three self-propelled artillery regiments of 3rd Division, followed.

As the flotilla of small craft neared the shore, the rocket-carrying LCT(R)s opened fire, concentrating their salvoes of 1,064 5in. projectiles on Queen Red and White sectors. Beach obstacles and close defences began to disappear under masses of flame and smoke. At a range of 7,000yds the self-propelled guns of the 3rd Division's field artillery, grouped in fours on their LCTs, opened fire and added their weight of high explosives to the bombardment.

When the LCTs carrying the amphibious Shermans reached a point 5,000yds from the beaches, they swung round to bring their bows downwind and unloaded their swimming tanks. Slowly the DD

Six miles offshore a flotilla of Landing Craft Assault (LCA) pass by the Assault Force 'S' Headquarters Ship, HMS *Largs*, on their way to Sword Beach. Each of the small craft carries 30 fully laden troops from the assault companies of 8th Brigade. In the foreground is a Landing Craft Tank with five Sherman DD tanks of the 13th/18th Hussars. These amphibious tanks will be launched much closer to shore, at about 5,000yds from the beach. (Imperial War Museum, A 23846)

HMS *Eglinton*

HMS *Kelvin*

HMS *Virago*

HMS *Verulam*

HMS *Serapis*

Destroyers bombarding beach defences, 3,000–6,000 yards offshore

HMS *Scourge*

HMS *Middleton*

HMS *Salzak*

HMS *Stord*

HMS *Scorpion*

HMS *Danae*

HMS *Dragon*

HMS *Frobisher*

Cruisers bombarding coastal artillery sites at Colleville, Ouistreham and Riva Bella, 5–7 miles offshore

Landing Craft Tank (Rocket) fire salvos of 8 inch rocket projectiles onto the area of Queen, White and Red beaches and the roads backing onto the sea front, from 5,000 yards offshore

OBOE

RED

GREEN

WHITE

RED

PETER

SWORD

QUEEN

GREEN

WHITE

RED

RESERVE BRIGADE

INTERMEDIATE BRIGADE

ASSAULT BRIGADE

ROGER

GREEN

WHITE

RED

P

O

N

M

L

K

J

I

H

G

F

E

D

C

B

A

Luc sur Mer

N

Lion-sur-Mer

41 RM Commando

La Brèche

1 South Lancs

2 East Yorks

Colleville-Plage

Riva-Bella

4 Commando

Orne

Cresserons

Hermanville

1 South Lancs

1 Special Service

2 East Yorks

Ouistreham

Plumetot

Colleville

Legend:
- Infantry
- Armour and self propelled artillery
- Commandos
- Support vehicles

0 — 1,000 yds
0 — 1,000 m

ASSAULT BRIGADE, landing from H Hour to H Hour + 120 minutes

A. 13/18 Hussars (DD tanks), 27 Armoured Brigade
   22 Dragoons, 79 Armoured Division
   Westminster Dragoons, 79 Armoured Division
   5 Assault Regiment Royal Engineers, 79 Armoured Division
B. Assault Companies, 1 South Lancs and 2 East Yorks, 8 Brigade
C. 7 Field Regiment Royal Artillery, 3 Division (Self Propelled Guns)
   33 Field Regiment Royal Artillery, 3 Division (Self Propelled Guns)
   76 Field Regiment Royal Artillery, 3 Division (Self Propelled Guns)
D. Follow-up Companies, 1 South Lancs and 2 East Yorks, 8 Brigade
E. 4 Commando, 41 RM Commando
F. 8 Brigade priority vehicles and 79 Division's wading tanks
G. Reserve Battalion, 1 Suffolk Regiment, 8 Brigade
H. Remainder 1 Special Service Brigade
I. 8 Brigade priority vehicles and stores

INTERMEDIATE BRIGADE, landing from H Hour + 150 minutes to H Hour + 250 minutes

J. 2 King's Shropshire Light Infantry, 185 Brigade
K. The Staffordshire Yeomanry, 27 Armoured Brigade
L. 2 Royal Warwickshire Regiment
   1 Royal Norfolk Regiment
M. 185 Brigade priority vehicles and stores

RESERVE BRIGADE, landing from H Hour + 270 minutes to H Hour + 360 minutes

N. 2 Lincolnshire Regiment, 9 Brigade
   1 King's Own Scottish Light Infantry, 9 Brigade
   2 Royal Ulster Rifles, 9 Brigade
O. 1 East Riding Yeomanry, 27 Armoured Brigade
P. 9 Brigade priority vehicles and stores

Further bombardment provided from assault craft
1. Landing Craft Flak (LCF)
2. 3 Division's self propelled artillery on board Landing Craft Tank (LCT)

A landing-craft approaches the shore close to the extreme right edge of Queen Red Beach. A Crab flail tank of 22nd Dragoons has been hit and is burning fiercely. Other tanks from 79th Armoured Division are on the beach, as is an armoured bulldozer. A few men are lying in the surf. In the sea can be seen some of the beach obstacles constructed by the enemy. The two prominent villas in the right background still exist, enabling this shot to be located as to the right of strongpoint 'Cod'. (Imperial War Museum, B5111)

Shermans of 13th/18th Hussars began to disembark down the steep ramps and into the choppy sea. Of the 40 amphibious vehicles in the LCTs, 34 were successfully launched. However, almost immediately waves began to slop over their floatation screens. The DD Shermans offered a very low freeboard to the foaming sea and quickly began to take in water. Their pumps worked at full capacity to try to keep the tanks afloat, but two succumbed to the sea and sank, drowning most of their crews.

In the assault landing-craft the more curious infantrymen peered over the sides to catch a glimpse of the faint shoreline of France looming ahead, only to watch it gradually disappear in a mass of black smoke and belching flame as the Allied bombardment continued to strike home. The choppy seas tossed the small assault boats around and the helmsmen had difficulty keeping station. Men were being seasick everywhere.

Ahead of the LCAs, continuing to plow their lonely way through the white crested waves, were the swimming tanks of the 13th/18th Hussars. These frail-looking amphibious tanks were almost invisible to the heavy LCTs coming up behind them. Some rockets from the landing-craft were starting to fall short, causing the LCTs to take evasive action, veering from their course and plunging amongst the swimming tanks. One DD Sherman was rammed and sunk, taking most of its crew with it.

The enemy had by now realised that an amphibious landing was taking place and began to retaliate. All along the beachfront the German guns opened up with counter-fire aimed at the approaching landing-craft. This began to fall amongst the leading vessels, forcing them to try to escape the screaming high-explosive shells. Within a few minutes the steady formations of Allied ships closing on the beaches began to break up, with craft weaving in and out of the partially submerged obstacles and trying to dodge enemy fire. Inexorably, the

sion pressed on, closing rapidly on the belt of breaking surf that
rked the shoreline.

At 0724hrs the infantry approached the final few yards of the run-in.
ngside and in front of them the first of the DD tanks began to touch
tom and grind their way up the sandy beach. Of the planned
anks, 31 had made it to the shore. Many of these, however, had their
ines drowned as their trim changed as they beached, but their guns
e, nevertheless, useful against enemy strongpoints until the
oming tide swamped them. At the end of the assault, 23 of the DD
ks had survived the battle. At 0725hrs the infantry hit the beach.

Coincidental with the arrival of the 13th/18th's amphibious
rmans, the LCTs bringing the specialised armour of the assault
up from 79th Armoured Division also landed. These tanks, which
e drawn from units of 22nd Dragoons, Westminster Dragoons and
Assault Regiment Royal Engineers, were armed with a variety of
cialised equipment and their tasks were many. Other equipment
h as bulldozers and 'Bullshorn' ploughs also arrived to deal with
ch and underwater obstacles.

According to the assault plan, the DD tanks would land just before the
antry and Royal Engineer teams in order to engage the enemy with their
nm guns as the others came ashore. However, the heavy seas had slowed
wn their approach and all three groups arrived more or less together.
tching intently from their concrete emplacements were the enemy
ops who had survived the bombardment and, once the barrage lifted to
w the attacking British troops to land, they began to emerge from their
lters. Although they were suffering from the shock of the rocket and
ll fire, their casualties seemed to be light. The first waves of the assault

**Commandos approach Sword
Beach in a Landing Craft Infantry
(Small) that has carried them
over the Channel. They will
disembark down the stepped
ramps in the foreground, which
will be lowered from the bows
into the shallow water. Ahead, on
the beach, drifting smoke helps
hide the concentration of
stranded armour. Tanks from
27th Armoured Brigade and
79th Armoured Division cluster
at the water's edge; some had
been knocked out whilst others
seek a way off of the beach.
(Imperial War Museum, B5102)**

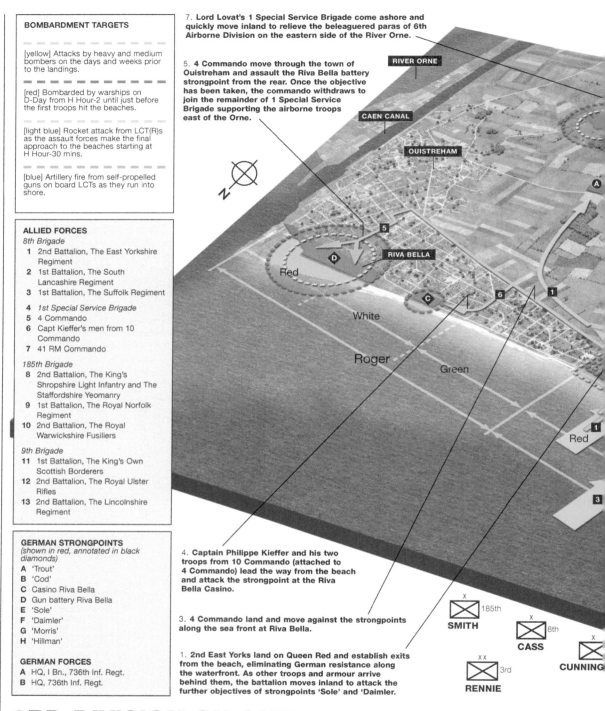

BOMBARDMENT TARGETS

▬▬▬ [yellow] Attacks by heavy and medium bombers on the days and weeks prior to the landings.

▬▬▬ [red] Bombarded by warships on D-Day from H Hour-2 until just before the first troops hit the beaches.

▬▬▬ [light blue] Rocket attack from LCT(R)s as the assault forces make the final approach to the beaches starting at H Hour-30 mins.

▬▬▬ [blue] Artillery fire from self-propelled guns on board LCTs as they run into shore.

ALLIED FORCES

8th Brigade
1 2nd Battalion, The East Yorkshire Regiment
2 1st Battalion, The South Lancashire Regiment
3 1st Battalion, The Suffolk Regiment

4 *1st Special Service Brigade*
5 4 Commando
6 Capt Kieffer's men from 10 Commando
7 41 RM Commando

185th Brigade
8 2nd Battalion, The King's Shropshire Light Infantry and The Staffordshire Yeomanry
9 1st Battalion, The Royal Norfolk Regiment
10 2nd Battalion, The Royal Warwickshire Fusiliers

9th Brigade
11 1st Battalion, The King's Own Scottish Borderers
12 2nd Battalion, The Royal Ulster Rifles
13 2nd Battalion, The Lincolnshire Regiment

GERMAN STRONGPOINTS
(shown in red, annotated in black diamonds)
A 'Trout'
B 'Cod'
C Casino Riva Bella
D Gun battery Riva Bella
E 'Sole'
F 'Daimler'
G 'Morris'
H 'Hillman'

GERMAN FORCES
A HQ, I Bn., 736th Inf. Regt.
B HQ, 736th Inf. Regt.

7. **Lord Lovat's 1 Special Service Brigade come ashore and quickly move inland to relieve the beleaguered paras of 6th Airborne Division on the eastern side of the River Orne.**

5. **4 Commando move through the town of Ouistreham and assault the Riva Bella battery strongpoint from the rear. Once the objective has been taken, the commando withdraws to join the remainder of 1 Special Service Brigade supporting the airborne troops east of the Orne.**

4. **Captain Philippe Kieffer and his two troops from 10 Commando (attached to 4 Commando) lead the way from the beach and attack the strongpoint at the Riva Bella Casino.**

3. **4 Commando land and move against the strongpoints along the sea front at Riva Bella.**

1. **2nd East Yorks land on Queen Red and establish exits from the beach, eliminating German resistance along the waterfront. As other troops and armour arrive behind them, the battalion moves inland to attack the further objectives of strongpoints 'Sole' and 'Daimler.**

RIVER ORNE
CAEN CANAL
OUISTREHAM
RIVA BELLA
Red
White
Roger
Green
Red

SMITH 185th

CASS 8th

CUNNING

RENNIE 3rd

3RD DIVISION ON QUEEN RED AND QUEEN WHITE BEACHES

6 June 1944, 0725hrs–1500hrs, viewed from the northwest showing landings by 8th Brigade, 3rd Division's assault brigade, and the battle to subdue strongpoint 'Cod' and secure the beachhead. As the follow-up brigades land Allied forces push inland expanding the lodgement and attacking a series of German strongpoints.

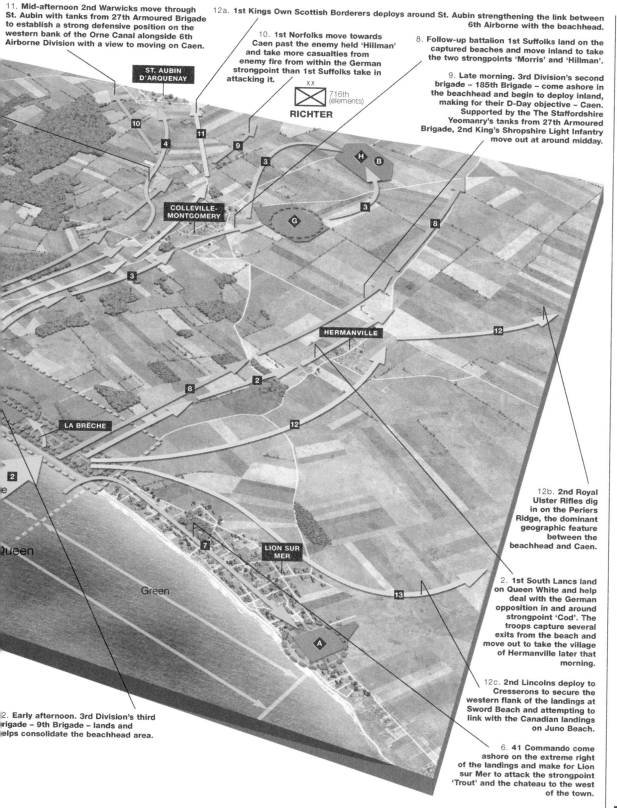

11. **Mid-afternoon 2nd Warwicks move through St. Aubin with tanks from 27th Armoured Brigade to establish a strong defensive position on the western bank of the Orne Canal alongside 6th Airborne Division with a view to moving on Caen.**

12a. **1st Kings Own Scottish Borderers deploys around St. Aubin strengthening the link between the beachhead and 6th Airborne with the beachhead.**

10. **1st Norfolks move towards Caen past the enemy held 'Hillman' and take more casualties from enemy fire from within the German strongpoint than 1st Suffolks take in attacking it.**

8. **Follow-up battalion 1st Suffolks land on the captured beaches and move inland to take the two strongpoints 'Morris' and 'Hillman'.**

9. **Late morning. 3rd Division's second brigade – 185th Brigade – come ashore in the beachhead and begin to deploy inland, making for their D-Day objective – Caen. Supported by the The Staffordshire Yeomanry's tanks from 27th Armoured Brigade, 2nd King's Shropshire Light Infantry move out at around midday.**

X X
716th (elements)
RICHTER

ST. AUBIN D'ARQUENAY

COLLEVILLE-MONTGOMERY

HERMANVILLE

LA BRÈCHE

LION SUR MER

Queen

Green

12b. **2nd Royal Ulster Rifles dig in on the Periers Ridge, the dominant geographic feature between the beachhead and Caen.**

2. **1st South Lancs land on Queen White and help deal with the German opposition in and around strongpoint 'Cod'. The troops capture several exits from the beach and move out to take the village of Hermanville later that morning.**

12c. **2nd Lincolns deploy to Cresserons to secure the western flank of the landings at Sword Beach and attempting to link with the Canadian landings on Juno Beach.**

6. **41 Commando come ashore on the extreme right of the landings and make for Lion sur Mer to attack the strongpoint 'Trout' and the chateau to the west of the town.**

2. **Early afternoon. 3rd Division's third brigade – 9th Brigade – lands and helps consolidate the beachhead area.**

55

infantry from British 8th Brigade touched down into mounting chaos as the larger LCTs and smaller LCAs vied for an open run-in to the beach. As they stormed ashore the infantry presented individual targets to the enemy troops and they responded with small-arms and mortar fire. Men began dropping as German machine gun fire ripped through the bunched groups of troops leaving the landing-craft.

'A' Company of the 1st South Lancs landed to the right on Queen White beach close by strongpoint 'Cod', which was itself an objective of the 2nd East Yorks who were landing to the left on Queen Red. 'A' Company of the South Lancs immediately took severe casualties from the German small-arms fire coming from the sprawling group of fortifications. The company commander and another officer were soon killed, but the remainder of the men quickly regrouped and moved to the right towards Lion sur Mer, clearing the houses along the shore. 'C' Company, landing alongside them, attacked the strongpoint that was giving so much trouble, helped by the East Yorks who were landing on Queen Red. The follow-up company of the South Lancs, 'B' Company, landed to the left of its assigned position and disembarked right opposite 'Cod' itself. Its men quickly threw themselves into a frontal assault on the wire fortifications and concrete emplacements surrounding the strongpoint. Resistance was fierce and casualties were heavy. 'B' Company's commander was killed, as was the battalion commander, Lieutenant-Colonel Burbury, when he landed a short while later.

Over to the left, the 2nd East Yorks touched down on Queen Red beach straight into a welter of machine gun and mortar fire. Even heavier fire criss-crossed the shoreline from 88mm and 75mm guns firing along the length of the beach from the protected confines of their concrete gun emplacements located on the edge of the dunes. Fire was returned by the tanks of 13th/18th Hussars together with the gun tanks of 22nd Dragoons and the Westminster Dragoons, but they too suffered many direct hits. The East Yorks had landed to the left of strongpoint 'Cod' and keenly felt the intense small-arms fire that came from its fortifications. One company assisted the infantry of the South Lancs in attacking the site, working its way around to infiltrate the area from the rear. After a fierce struggle 'Cod' was eventually overcome and cleared.

Coming ashore just behind the leading infantry were the obstacle clearing teams charged with removing beach obstructions to clear the way for the follow-up landing-craft. Their work was exhausting and dangerous, and the men, who were forced to work in the open, were vulnerable to enemy fire, incoming landing-craft and the swirling surf. They had great difficulty clearing paths through the obstacles, for each ramp, pole, steel hedgehog and concrete tetrahedron seemed to be armed with a Teller mine or an impact-detonated anti-aircraft shell. The obstacle clearing teams worked feverishly against an incoming tide blown on by high winds. As the minutes passed the water gradually overwhelmed them and their work, and then the next wave arrived.

Crashing through the obstacles and dodging landing-craft from the assault wave came the 24 landing-craft carrying the first of the commandos from Lord Lovat's 1st Special Service Brigade and 41 (Royal Marine) Commando from Brigadier Leicester's 4th Special Service Brigade.

The men of 4 Commando were landed on the extreme left side of Queen Red beach with the objective of clearing the strongpoint of the

OVERLEAF **No. 4 COMMANDO MOVES INLAND**
Troops from No 4 Commando moving along the lateral road behind Sword beach, advancing towards the gun battery at Ouistreham/Riva Bella. As they advanced the commandos came under mortar and sniper fire. Captain Kieffer's contingent of French commandos led the attack inland and moved ahead to clear the strongpoint at the Ouistreham Casino. To the right of the commandos a group of the 2nd East Yorks pause briefly during their advance on German strongpoint 'Sole' to shelter behind a DD Sherman tank of the 13th/18th Royal Hussars. By this time resistance along the beach was beginning to wane and enemy troops were withdrawing in the face of the massed Allied infantry coming ashore. The leading elements of British 3rd Division came under increasing fire from enemy pockets and rearguards. The German 716th Division had lost much of its cohesion and individuals and small groups were retiring towards Caen attempting to regroup and re-establish contact with their regiment. Captain Keiffer's men were attached to No 4 Commando for the invasion, but formed part of No 10 Inter-Allied Commando, a unit composed entirely of men from countries which were under Nazi occupation. No 10 Commando included Dutch, French, Belgian, Norwegian and Polish Troops, and even had an X-Troop of men from Germany itself. Kieffer's two French Troops joined No 4 Commando specifically for the Normandy landings and were given the honour of being the first commandos to land on their home soil. These Frenchmen remained in action throughout June and July when, along with No 4 Commando, they crossed over the River Orne to join MajGen Gale's 6th Airborne Division in the defence of the left flank. No. 4 Commando was a very experienced unit and had been one of the first of the

56

s picture was taken a short
le after the assault waves
 landed. Some vehicles are
 the beach and onto the
eral road at the rear. Smoke
m burning buildings drifts over
 beaches, helping to mask the
dings. (Imperial War Museum,
25)

Casino at Riva Bella and eliminating the gun battery on the beach at Ouistreham/Riva Bella. Commanded by Lieutenant-Colonel Dawson, 4 Commando landed straight into a barrage of intense small-arms fire, which pinned them to the beach for some moments. By this time the East Yorks should have had the beach clear for the commandos to move through, but opposition from 'Cod' and the surrounding dunes had delayed progress. As a result, the commandos had to fight their way off the beach and onto the lateral road leading to Ouistreham, which ran behind the waterfront.

Also landing at this time was 41 RM Commando. It touched down 300yds to the right of its allocated position on the extreme western end of Queen White beach. Its task was to eliminate the strongpoint 'Trout' in Lion sur Mer and attack the chateau west of the town. It was also to link up with the remainder of 4th Special Service Brigade who were landing on Juno Beach away to the west, thus joining together the two landing beaches. The elimination of the radar station at Douvres was a secondary objective. The Royal Marine commandos managed to get off Queen White without too much difficulty and then its force split into two groups, one attacking the chateau, whilst the other moved against 'Trout'. By the end of the morning it had cleared Lion sur Mer – the strongpoint at 'Trout' was deserted – and attacked the chateau. This latter objective was, however, a difficult proposition, and the group attacking the chateau lost its commander and two troop commanders killed. Enemy resistance was such that it was found to be impossible to advance westwards from the town to link up with Juno Beach that day. Similarly, 41 RM Commando did not have the strength to attack the radar station at Douvres.

With the help of the tanks from 13th/18th Hussars and infantry from the newly arrived follow-up battalion, the 1st Suffolks, British 8th

). 4 COMMANDO CONTINUED
ecial forces to be raised. It had
eviously taken part in several
ds on enemy held territory, the
st notable of which was the
eration at Dieppe in August
42, when it attacked and
stroyed the German battery at
rengeville, the only successful
rt of the whole operation. It
ent on to take part in the
ndings at Walcheren in
lland in November 1944.
oward Gerrard)

This picture was taken at around 0845hrs near the junction of Queen Red and White beaches opposite German strongpoint 'Cod'. In the foreground are two Royal Engineers from a Beach Group who can be identified by their white banded helmets and their sleeve badges that depict a red anchor on a white background. Troops of 41 Royal Marine Commando assemble in the mid-background ready for their move on Lion sur Mer. In the far background, troops of 2nd Middlesex Regiment, the 3rd Division's machine gun battalion, make their way across the tidal stretch of beach, taking casualties as they move. (Imperial War Museum, B5114)

Brigade gradually began to clear gaps and open exits from Quee Beach. Flail tanks swept routes through minefields and bridging tank spanned anti-tank traps and ditches to allow the infantry to move inland The division's self-propelled artillery had landed and joined the infant of 8th Brigade to support the advance. More armour arrived a little late when the next regiment of 27th Armour Brigade, the Staffordshir Yeomanry, began to come ashore. By 0900hrs 1st South Lancs ha pressed south and secured the village of Hermanville, and the 2nd Ea Yorkshires had also moved off the beach, advancing towards the Germa position 'Sole'.

With the beach reasonably clear of localised opposition, 1st Suffolk now began to move inland towards the village of Colleville and the tw strongpoints of 'Morris' and 'Hillman'. Behind them the incoming tide made stronger by an onshore wind, had pushed the sea up almost to th dunes. The width of the beach had been narrowed to just a small strip often only 30yds wide. With the imminent arrival of more landing-craf bringing increasing numbers of troops, tanks, guns and transport, th water's edge became a scene of chaos and disorder. Traffic jams bega to grow at the exits and it took all the skills of the beach masters t extricate each new unit from the mêlée. As a result, the intermediat brigade of 3rd Division, 185th Brigade, had few tanks available t support its vitally important attack towards Caen when it arrived o Queen beach. In an effort to maintain momentum, 185th Brigade'

commander, Brigadier Smith, gave the order for the leading battalion, 2nd King's Shropshire Light Infantry, to start its move without the support of the Staffordshire Yeomanry, hoping that the tanks might extricate themselves from the queues around the beach exits and join them later.

Meanwhile, 4 Commando had moved along the lateral road behind the beach and was attacking its objectives along the seafront at Ouistreham and Riva Bella from the rear. The strongpoint at the Casino was assaulted by two troops from 10 Commando who were attached to 4 Commando. These two troops of Frenchmen commanded by Captain Phillippe Kieffer, were given the independent task of reducing the Casino strongpoint, making the attack a purely French one. They were also given the honour of advancing first, leading 4 Commando off the beach and down the road into Ouistreham. At a rendezvous point behind the dunes they dumped their rucksacks and prepared for their attack.

The seaside Casino at Riva Bella had been completely demolished by the Germans and a strongpoint built around its rubble. It consisted of interlocking defensive bunkers and machine-gun posts, trenches, wire entanglements and minefields. Most of the site was below ground or in field works, with few structures visible to the attacking commandos. Kieffer split his men into two groups and attacked the fortifications from the rear at two different points. It was a battle of small arms, hand grenades and personal anti-tank weapons. The two groups infiltrated between buildings close by, firing as they went. A large bunker on the left, topped by a steel cupola, proved to be a difficult proposition, while 50mm anti-tank guns firing through concrete embrasures made the task still more difficult. Nothing that the Frenchmen had in their armoury had any effect on these structures and the casemates proved to be a problem during the whole of the attack, as was a water tower on the right, which overlooked the position. After 30 minutes of fighting, and

Sword Beach, Queen Red sector, some time after the initial assault. A medic attends to wounded commandos in the shelter of an Armoured Vehicle Royal Engineer (AVRE) from 79th Assault Squadron RE, part of 5th Assault Regiment RE. The tank is a Churchill armed with a 'Petard' – a 12in. calibre weapon capable of firing a 26lb charge of high explosive over 200yds against concrete emplacements and steel obstacles. In the right background is a M10 Wolverine tank-destroyer, probably from 20th Anti-tank Regiment RA. (Imperial War Museum, B5095)

British dead on Sword Beach lie scattered in front of the wire defences surrounding strongpoint 'Cod'. (Imperial War Museum, B5118)

with mounting casualties weakening their fire power, the attack of Kieffer's men stalled. Just as Kieffer had decided to make a last desperate attempt at charging the strongpoint, word came through that there were several DD tanks in the streets of Ouistreham. The young captain went off to search for one to support his attack and later returned riding on top of a Sherman. Under his direction the tank knocked out the anti-tank guns and water tower and silenced the bunker. With these obstacles removed, the remainder of Kieffer's men were able to clear the enemy out of the trenches and dugouts that made up the strongpoint.

Further away to the east, the remainder of 4 Commando closed on the rear of the gun battery near the mouth of the River Orne. The guns were housed in open emplacements on the beach within a heavily fortified site. The area around the battery was, like the Casino position, thick with minefields, wire entanglements and trench systems. Machine guns covered every approach and 50mm anti-tank guns watched over the landward side of the perimeter. About 100yds short of the gun positions was an angled anti-tank ditch. Dominating the whole site was a large concrete tower that housed the control and ranging instruments for the coastal guns. The tower was 17m high and looked down on every approach, but was not built as an offensive structure and so, apart from the large observation slit on the seaward side at the top, had very few openings through which weapons could be fired. The greatest danger presented by the structure were the showers of hand grenades thrown from the parapet as the commandos passed by underneath. Built to withstand the very worst bombing and shelling, the tower remained intact and was not finally taken until a few days later. The commandos were content to leave it for the follow-up troops, who would have more time to invest in its capture.

The men of 4 Commando attacked the gun emplacements in a series of short fire fights linked by bouts of rapid movement, never allowing the momentum to slacken. They came at the enemy from all angles. Passing from cover to cover through the bomb craters, firing as they ran, they were soon amongst the trenches, sweeping along them with light machine gun fire and grenades. Enemy return fire came at the commandos from all directions; from machine gun posts dotted around the edge of the fortified area and from the observation slit at the top of the tower. As the commandos closed on the artillery emplacements it soon became clear that the sites were empty of weapons. The guns had been removed earlier by the Germans and transported inland. It was, therefore, pointless to continue with the attack and 4 Commando withdrew back into Ouistreham to regroup and join the remainder of 1st Special Service Brigade.

Following behind the landings made by 4 Commando and sandwiched between the arrival of 8th Brigade's reserve battalion and 3rd Division's priority vehicles, came the remainder of Lord Lovat's 1st Special Service Brigade. Brigadier Lord Lovat brought his brigade ashore on Queen Red and immediately sent 6 Commando ahead to relieve British 6th Airborne Division to the east of the River Orne. A signaller had picked up the message that the two bridges over the river and the canal at Bénouville had been captured intact and this boosted the commandos spitits. They knew that they had to make haste to relieve the beleaguered paratroopers, but the advance was difficult. The commandos had to fight their way through a series of enemy positions, overcoming four strongpoints and a four-gun artillery battery on the way. Nonetheless, they arrived at Bénouville just two and a half minutes behind schedule, to the great joy of LtCol Pine Coffin and his 7th Parachute Battalion. Then came the rest of the brigade, with Lord Lovat leading the way with his personal piper, Bill Millin, playing as they marched. Once over the two bridges, Lovat's Brigade was sent to the northern end of 6th Airborne's positions to hold the high ground around Le Plein and the surrounding villages.

By late morning, 3rd Division had landed the whole of Brig Smith's 185th Brigade and two of the three armoured regiments from 27th Armoured Brigade, although some parts of these units were still immobile on the beaches, snarled in massive traffic jams. Brigadier Smith had brought the leading elements of his brigade south to Hermanville and had sent 2nd KSLI forward on foot, pushing out towards Caen supported by the self-propelled guns of 7th Field Regiment. By the time the battalion had reached the lower slopes of Periers Ridge, the tanks of the Staffordshire Yeomanry had caught up. Periers Ridge should have been in Allied hands by then, for 8th Brigade had originally planned to move onto the feature quite early in the battle, but 1st South Lancs had dug in at Hermanville and halted their advance.

The drive for Caen was supposed to be, after the establishment of a successful beachhead, the most important objective for 3rd Division on 6 June. General Montgomery had planned to have Caen under his control by the end of the day. He needed the town to anchor his left flank and provide a stop line which any German armoured counter-attack would either have to travel through or bypass. The road network converging on the city was of vital strategic importance both for the build-up of strength and for future expansion out of the lodgement areas. The importance of the capture of Caen, however, seems to have

LEFT **Sword Beach Queen Red sector as it is today; the beach is still lined with the dunes behind which men of the 2nd East Yorks took shelter during the first minutes of the assault. In the mid-distance is the site of strongpoint 'Cod'. (Ken Ford)**

BELOW **A German aerial reconnaissance view of the Orne estuary taken on 28 June looking towards Ouistreham. Certain intelligence comments have been added: at the top, numbers '2' and '16' identify sunken freighters; 'B' shows a landing-strip under construction; 'C' shows a line of 15 tents; 'D' shows landing zones with over 100 gliders identified; and 'E' locates Bailey bridges that have been put across the River Orne and the Caen Canal. (Bundesarchiv, 1U1/2191)**

been regarded with less urgency by those on the ground, and emphasis seems to have been placed on consolidation rather than expansion. It was an understandable approach, for although a firm foothold had been gained, the situation was still extremely fluid, with some areas seemingly open for the taking, whilst others had to be fought for against a tenacious and well-entrenched enemy.

The other two battalions of 185th Brigade had also begun their drive on Caen: 1st Norfolks were passing through the 1st Suffolks strung out in Colleville, and 2nd Warwickshires were progressing through St Aubin in the rear of Lovat's Brigade. The 1st Norfolks took heavy casualties when it emerged from Colleville and moved out into open countryside across the eastern flank of strongpoint 'Hillman'. Accurate small-arms and artillery fire from the feature caused the battalion over 150 casualties.

At that time, 'Hillman' was in the process of being cleared by the advance companies of the 1st Suffolks. The battalion had already overcome enemy resistance in Colleville and in the strongpoint at 'Morris', and it was now attempting to do the same at 'Hillman'. It was a formidable task, for the subterranean fortified area housed the headquarters of Oberst Ludwig Krug's 736th Infantry Regiment. The strongpoint covered an area 600yds by 400yds and contained two H605 concrete emplacements topped by steel cupolas, numerous concrete shelters, anti-tank guns and 'Tobruk' machine gun pits. It was surrounded by barbed wire entanglements and an extensive minefield. Air bombardment and shell fire from warships had done little to dampen its offensive spirit.

The outer wire was breached with bangalore torpedoes by 'D' Company of the Suffolks. Then came the minefield and the inner belt of wire. Eventually the central area was entered by the infantry. Once inside the wire, the steel cupolas were attacked by 17-pdr anti-tank weapons, but the shells made little impact on the solid round structures. The enemy garrison were bottled up inside the strongpoint in their underground bunkers, but their small-arms fire was very troublesome to the British infantry on the surface. One by one the Suffolks knocked out the anti-tank guns and eliminated a good number of the surface

entaur tank on a stand close to egasus Bridge. The tank came shore on D-Day and belonged to th (Independent) Battery of the oyal Marine Armoured Support roup. It arrived on Queen Beach t La Brèche and was knocked ut shortly after landing. (en Ford)

**THE CAPTURE OF STRONGPOINT
HILLMAN.** Men of 1st Suffolks
pass a knocked-out 5cm KwK in
an open emplacement. The crew
are dead around it, killed by
artillery fire earlier in the attack.
The Germans mounted large
numbers of these former tank
guns in defences along the
caost. The gun had a range of
around 6,500 metres with a rate
of fire of between 15 and
20 rounds per minute. The main
problem faced by the Suffolks in
silencing the strongpoint was
that virtually all of it was housed
underground. Surface
emplacements could be attacked
with support weapons, but
the machine guns housed in
well-protected subterranean
fortifications were a more
difficult nut to crack. Once
through the outer wire and
minefields and onto the surface
of the strongpoint, the troops
were exposed to concentrated
small arms fire from almost
impregnable positions. Once a
route through the minefields had
been cleared for the armour the
tanks enabled the infantry to
close with the emplacements
and attack them with explosives.
It was still a difficult task,
however, as the shells from the

machine gun pits, but fire continued to come at them from
directions and from every dip in the ground. Tanks arrived and join
in the action, enabling the infantry to close on the trench systems, b
it was a slow process to overcome each enemy infantryman in h
well-concealed hiding place. Mopping up and eliminating eve
emplacement went on for hours. In some cases the bunkers had to
blown out with heavy charges placed right up against their entrances
the battalion's pioneers. It took until 2015hrs that evening befo
Oberst Krug and his men were finally winkled out of their undergrou
bunkers. By then it was too late for the Suffolks to move any clos
towards Caen, so they consolidated where they were for the night.

The reserve brigade of 3rd Division was 9th Infantry Brigade, whic
landed in the early afternoon but took a considerable time to extrica
itself from the log jam on the beaches and move inland. The thre
infantry battalions advanced from the seafront on the right of th
lodgement with the intention of concentrating in the area of Plumeto
close by Periers Ridge. Brigadier Cunningham's orders were to take h
brigade straight down the right flank towards Carpiquet airfield an
Caen, but when he met the divisional commander, MajGen Rennie, an
I Corps' commander, LtGen Crocker, on the outskirts of Hermanvill
he was told that the role of his brigade had changed. Because
the pressure being applied to the 6th Airborne by 21st Panzer Divisio
his brigade was to move over to the left and assist MajGen Gale
beleaguered paratroopers.

The armour allocated to support 9th Brigade, 1st East Ridir
Yeomanry from 27th Armoured Brigade, had not yet landed, so Renn
told Cunningham to wait until these tanks were ashore before movin
The brigadier then warned the 1st King's Own Scottish Borderers of th
change of plans and returned to his Brigade HQ to await the arrival o
his armour. Once there, he had the misfortune to be wounded by a stic
of mortar bombs, which killed six of his staff and injured another fiv

The brigade's second in command was not readily available as he was liaising with the Airborne Division and so continuity of command was lost at a crucial time. Lieutenant-Colonel Orr eventually assumed command of the brigade and found that the enemy on the right flank were more active than originally thought, so 9th Brigade would once again need to be involved there. As a result, 9th Brigade did little to help in the advance on Caen that day. The 2nd Lincolns consolidated a position facing the enemy in Cresserons to the right of Hermanville, 2nd Royal Ulster Rifles dug-in just outside of Hermanville on the lower slopes of the ridge and 1st KOSB moved across to hold the village of St Aubin.

The advance by 185th Brigade on Caen, which had begun with the move from Hermanville by 2nd KSLI without its tanks, developed into a powerful thrust when the Shermans of the Staffordshire Yeomanry joined up with the infantry, together with the self-propelled artillery of 7th and 33rd Field Regiments, the anti-tank guns of 41st Anti-tank Battery and a heavy machine gun platoon from 2nd Middlesex Regiment. Commanded by Lieutenant-Colonel Maurice, 2nd KSLI advanced up the left side of Periers Ridge, just to the right of the battle for the possession of 'Hillman'. On the reverse slope of the ridge, near Point 61, the battalion came into contact with an established battery of German artillery, which also housed the HQ of I Battalion 1716th Artillery Regiment and its commander, Major Hoff. The enemy put up a spirited fight, and the position was only taken after a good deal of resistance. Now feeling rather vulnerable with his right flank exposed to open country along Periers Ridge, LtCol Maurice decided to leave 'B' Squadron of the Staffordshire Yeomanry on the high ground to protect his advance from enemy interference from that quarter. With his position more secure, LtCol Maurice continued with his move on Caen, taking the villages of Beuville and Bieville and sending a company of infantry supported with tanks into Lebisey Wood close to the outskirts of the city.

The German reaction to the landings

German opposition to the landings on Sword Beach came from troops of Richter's 716th Infantry Division. The sector was manned by I Battalion, 736th Infantry Regiment around Ouistreham and III Battalion 736th Infantry Regiment in and behind Lion sur Mer. The guns in the area were crewed by troops from the division's I Battalion, 1716th Artillery Regiment. Many of these units contained a high percentage of foreign, mainly Eastern, volunteers who fought surprisingly well. Resistance everywhere in the invasion zone was quite stiff, especially when the defenders were protected by concrete and steel fortifications. German regulars and NCOs bolstered the resolve of these troops to the extent that almost every strongpoint and gun emplacement had to be seized by force, but the greater strength and fire power of the British troops engaged on Sword inevitably wore down the static defences. It might have been much worse if the German positions had been completed to the standard that Rommel would have liked. If more time and effort had been put into the building of the Atlantic Wall sooner, then the possibility of the British establishing a foothold on the coast of Normandy would have been in doubt.

When news of the airborne landings began to filter back to the German headquarters during the night, the High Command was

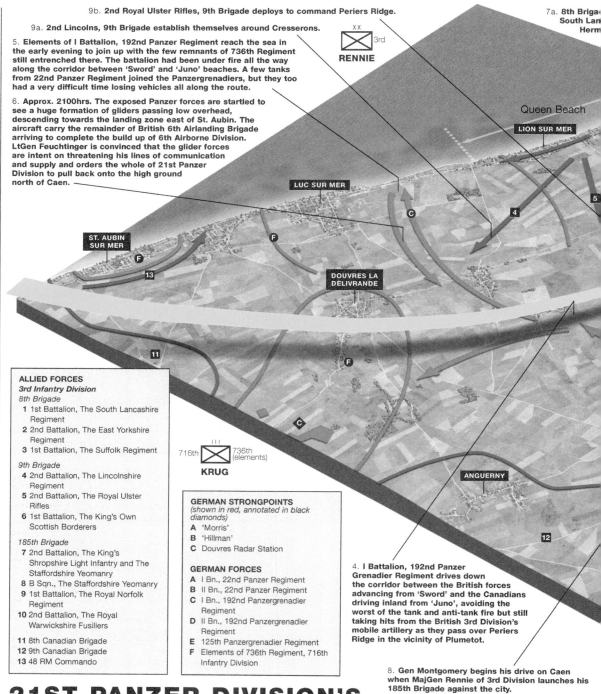

9b. 2nd Royal Ulster Rifles, 9th Brigade deploys to command Periers Ridge.

9a. 2nd Lincolns, 9th Brigade establish themselves around Cresserons.

5. Elements of I Battalion, 192nd Panzer Regiment reach the sea in the early evening to join up with the few remnants of 736th Regiment still entrenched there. The battalion had been under fire all the way along the corridor between 'Sword' and 'Juno' beaches. A few tanks from 22nd Panzer Regiment joined the Panzergrenadiers, but they too had a very difficult time losing vehicles all along the route.

6. Approx. 2100hrs. The exposed Panzer forces are startled to see a huge formation of gliders passing low overhead, descending towards the landing zone east of St. Aubin. The aircraft carry the remainder of British 6th Airlanding Brigade arriving to complete the build up of 6th Airborne Division. LtGen Feuchtinger is convinced that the glider forces are intent on threatening his lines of communication and supply and orders the whole of 21st Panzer Division to pull back onto the high ground north of Caen.

7a. 8th Briga... South Lan... Herm...

RENNIE — 3rd ╳╳

Queen Beach

LION SUR MER

LUC SUR MER

ST. AUBIN SUR MER

DOUVRES LA DÉLIVRANDE

ALLIED FORCES

3rd Infantry Division

8th Brigade
1 1st Battalion, The South Lancashire Regiment
2 2nd Battalion, The East Yorkshire Regiment
3 1st Battalion, The Suffolk Regiment

9th Brigade
4 2nd Battalion, The Lincolnshire Regiment
5 2nd Battalion, The Royal Ulster Rifles
6 1st Battalion, The King's Own Scottish Borderers

185th Brigade
7 2nd Battalion, The King's Shropshire Light Infantry and The Staffordshire Yeomanry
8 B Sqn., The Staffordshire Yeomanry
9 1st Battalion, The Royal Norfolk Regiment
10 2nd Battalion, The Royal Warwickshire Fusiliers
11 8th Canadian Brigade
12 9th Canadian Brigade
13 48 RM Commando

716th — 736th (elements)

KRUG

GERMAN STRONGPOINTS
(shown in red, annotated in black diamonds)
A 'Morris'
B 'Hillman'
C Douvres Radar Station

GERMAN FORCES
A I Bn., 22nd Panzer Regiment
B II Bn., 22nd Panzer Regiment
C I Bn., 192nd Panzergrenadier Regiment
D II Bn., 192nd Panzergrenadier Regiment
E 125th Panzergrenadier Regiment
F Elements of 736th Regiment, 716th Infantry Division

ANGUERNY

4. I Battalion, 192nd Panzer Grenadier Regiment drives down the corridor between the British forces advancing from 'Sword' and the Canadians driving inland from 'Juno', avoiding the worst of the tank and anti-tank fire but still taking hits from the British 3rd Division's mobile artillery as they pass over Periers Ridge in the vicinity of Plumetot.

8. Gen Montgomery begins his drive on Caen when MajGen Rennie of 3rd Division launches his 185th Brigade against the city.

21ST PANZER DIVISION'S COUNTERATTACK

6 June 1944, approx 1600hrs–2100hrs, viewed from the southwest showing the attack against the beachhead by LtGen Edgar Feuchtinger's 21st Panzer Division, including 192nd Panzergrenadier Regiment's drive to the coast near Lion sur Mer. With the support of its own self-propelled guns and elements of 27th Armoured Brigade, British 3rd Division blunts the attack and inflicts heavy casualties on the Panzer formations.

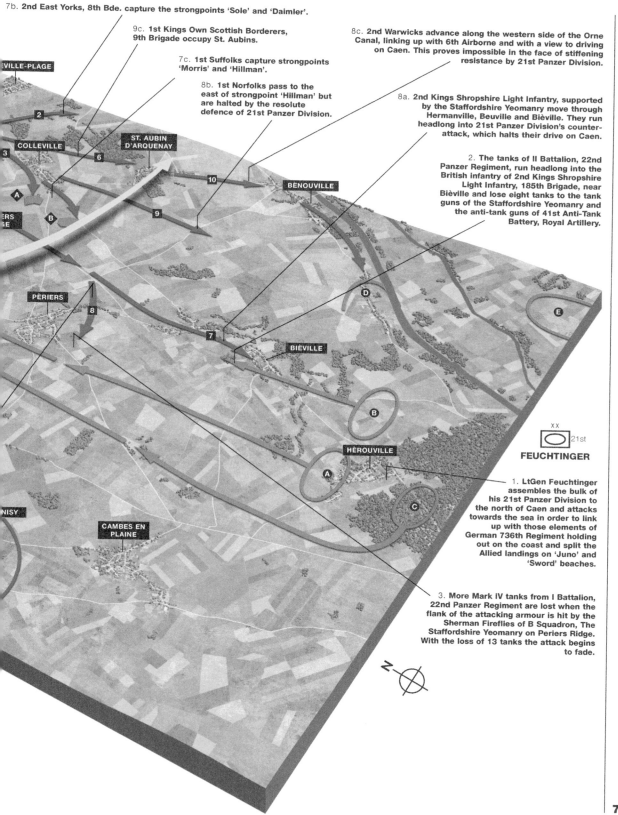

7b. **2nd East Yorks, 8th Bde. capture the strongpoints 'Sole' and 'Daimler'.**

9c. **1st Kings Own Scottish Borderers, 9th Brigade occupy St. Aubins.**

7c. **1st Suffolks capture strongpoints 'Morris' and 'Hillman'.**

8b. **1st Norfolks pass to the east of strongpoint 'Hillman' but are halted by the resolute defence of 21st Panzer Division.**

8c. **2nd Warwicks advance along the western side of the Orne Canal, linking up with 6th Airborne and with a view to driving on Caen. This proves impossible in the face of stiffening resistance by 21st Panzer Division.**

8a. **2nd Kings Shropshire Light Infantry, supported by the Staffordshire Yeomanry move through Hermanville, Beuville and Bièville. They run headlong into 21st Panzer Division's counter-attack, which halts their drive on Caen.**

2. **The tanks of II Battalion, 22nd Panzer Regiment, run headlong into the British infantry of 2nd Kings Shropshire Light Infantry, 185th Brigade, near Bièville and lose eight tanks to the tank guns of the Staffordshire Yeomanry and the anti-tank guns of 41st Anti-Tank Battery, Royal Artillery.**

VILLE-PLAGE

COLLEVILLE

ST. AUBIN D'ARQUENAY

BÉNOUVILLE

PÉRIERS

BIÉVILLE

HÉROUVILLE

CAMBES EN PLAINE

NISY

FEUCHTINGER

xx
□○ 21st

1. **LtGen Feuchtinger assembles the bulk of his 21st Panzer Division to the north of Caen and attacks towards the sea in order to link up with those elements of German 736th Regiment holding out on the coast and split the Allied landings on 'Juno' and 'Sword' beaches.**

3. **More Mark IV tanks from I Battalion, 22nd Panzer Regiment are lost when the flank of the attacking armour is hit by the Sherman Fireflies of B Squadron, The Staffordshire Yeomanry on Periers Ridge. With the loss of 13 tanks the attack begins to fade.**

N

uncertain whether the reported parachute activities were the start of the actual invasion or just a diversion to shift attention away from a larger force arriving elsewhere, probably in the area of the Pas de Calais. When details came of the size and scale of the seaborne landings, von Rundstedt knew that the long-awaited Allied invasion was taking place. He immediately asked Hitler for the release of the Panzer divisions that were being held specifically to counter this event. However, permission was slow in coming because Hitler and his Supreme Command HQ were convinced that the Normandy landings were just a feint. They did not think that it was time to release the Panzer reserves and told von Rundstedt to deal with the situation with the forces of Army Group B that were present in the region and the two Panzer divisions already in Normandy, the 12th SS and Panzer Lehr divisions.

Concrete anti-tank 'dragon's teeth' running alongside the beach huts to the rear of the Casino strongpoint at Riva Bella. The structures are some of the very few remains of the once powerful German beach fortification taken by Capt Phillippe Kieffer and his commandos on D-Day. (Ken Ford)

Generalfeldmarschall Rommel, commander of Army Group B, was at his home in Germany when he received news of the invasion and he was, therefore, not in a position to present his views to Hitler himself. Had he done so, he might have been able to convince the Führer that all available Panzer forces should attack the beaches and sweep the invaders back into the sea before they became established. As it was, the only tank force available to be used locally to counter the landings on D-Day was Feuchtinger's 21st Panzer Division, located to the south of Caen. By the time the armour of this division began to move against the beaches it was already mid-morning and Allied aircraft were patrolling the sky pouncing on any German road convoys.

COUNTER-ATTACK BY GERMAN 21st PANZER DIVISION

Sword Beach lay in the sector of German LXXXIV Corps, commanded by General der Artillerie Erich Marcks. He immediately saw that the main threat to the German defence of Normandy was the British capture of Caen, and he urged that an armoured counter-attack be launched. The intention was to reach the sea between the landings on Sword and Juno and then to sweep along the beaches to eliminate the Allied landings. Generalmajor Edgar Feuchtinger was ordered to send all available units of the 21st Panzer Division round to the northern edge of Caen to be assembled near Lebisey ready for the attack. This was the very point that the British 2nd KSLI were moving on, and at around 1600hrs the two sides met.

Up on the hill above Lebisey, Gen Marcks told the commander of 100th Panzer Regiment, Oberst von Oppeln-Bronikowski: 'Oppeln, if you don't succeed in throwing the British back into the sea, we shall have lost the war'. The young colonel then mounted his tank and ordered the advance to begin. Feuchtinger had assembled the two tank

A troop of commandos from 1st Special Service Brigade cross over a wire entanglement on the edge of the beach to move up to an assembly area prior to the long march to join up with the airborne troops on the eastern side of the River Orne. In the background a Churchill AVRE tank from 79th Armoured Division is carrying a small box girder bridge across the beach ready to lay it across an obstacle. (Imperial War Museum, B5071)

Commandos of 1st Special Service Brigade move off in single file, skirting a minefield as they go. The picture was taken at around 1000hrs on D-Day, just after the troops had assembled in groups and were moving inland to join up with the airborne. (Imperial War Museum, B5063)

battalions of 100th Panzer Regiment and the infantry of I Battalion of 192nd Panzergrenadier Regiment as his strike force. The tanks advanced on the right, whilst the mounted Panzergrenadiers took the left flank. Almost immediately the German advance ran into trouble.

Lieutenant-Colonel Maurice had been alerted to enemy tank movements ahead by 'Y' Company of his 2nd KSLI, who had moved into Lebisey Wood. The colonel quickly took steps to prepare for a counter-

attack, placing 'A' Squadron of the Staffordshire Yeomanry on his left and lining his front with his own 6-pdr anti-tank guns and the self-propelled guns of 41st Anti-tank Battery. When it began, the German attack came straight at him, with 40 or so PzKpfw IVs from 100th Panzer Regiment's II Battalion charging across his front. These tanks were met by a hail of fire that immediately knocked out four of them and damaged others. Reeling from such fierce resistance, the armour of 21st Panzer Division veered away to their left, but here they had the misfortune to encounter the Staffordshire Yeomanry's 17-pdr. guns of 'B' Squadron's Sherman Fireflies. More German tanks were knocked out. Still further over to the left, the regiment's I Battalion ran into the 105mm Priest self-propelled guns of 7th Field Regiment RA and still

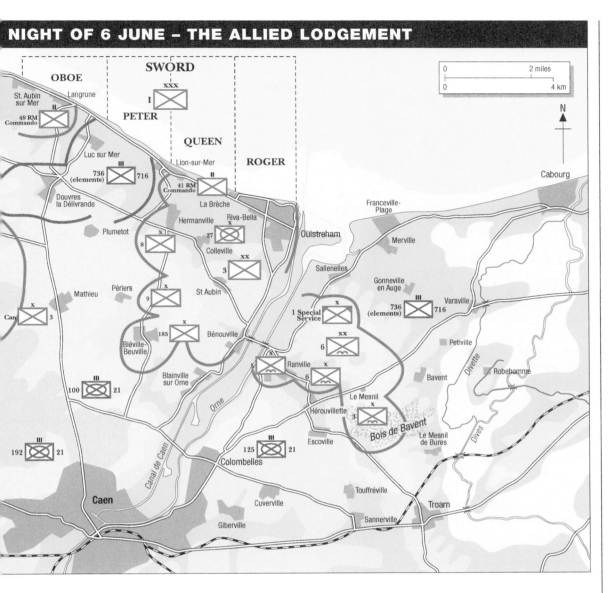

more hits were taken. After a short while the German armoured attack was in chaos. Thirteen tanks had been completely destroyed, while many more were damaged and co-ordination was lost.

The 192nd Panzergrenadiers fared slightly better. Advancing on the extreme left flank of the attack, the 192nd's route took it away from the main strength of 185th Brigade's guns, and it was able to cautiously pick its way over the western end of Periers Ridge, passing through the gap between the British 3rd Division and the Canadian landings on Juno Beach. Some of its strength was lost during the advance, but elements of I Battalion actually made their way to the sea to meet up with isolated pockets of the 736th Infantry Regiment, who were holding out near Lion sur Mer. These men were joined a little later by a few tanks of 100th Panzer Regiment's I Battalion. By this time it was early evening and these exposed units waited expectantly for fresh orders that would exploit their remarkable advance.

ABOVE **Strongpoint 'Hillman' was mostly built underground with a myriad of tunnels and bunkers invisible to troops on the surface. This picture shows one of the few entrances to the complex, guarded locally by 'Tobruk' weapons pits and machine gun embrasures. In the distance is a steel cupola, which housed a machine gun that resisted all British attempts to silence it. (Ken Ford)**

RIGHT **One of the two steel cupolas that formed the close defence of the objective code-named 'Hillman'. The open nature of the strongpoint can be clearly seen. With almost all of the complex underground, it was a difficult fortification to attack. (Ken Ford)**

Troops of 8th Brigade move
inland from the beaches past
a Sherman tank of the
13th/18th Royal Hussars. On the
road, supporting the move, are
M10 Wolverine tank-destroyers.
(Imperial War Museum, B5080)

However, no new orders came because Gen Feuchtinger had been alarmed by a new development taking place in the sky above him. At 2100hrs the air was filled with over 250 gliders and their tug aircraft carrying the 6th Airlanding Brigade to their landing zone near St Aubin. This landing was bringing Gen Gale's follow-up brigade to strengthen his hold east of the Orne. Feuchtinger was convinced that these air landings in the rear of his exposed division would eventually lead to its annihilation, and he gave the order for all units to consolidate north of Caen and produce a defensive line ringing the city. The new plan meant the withdrawal of the small force that had reached the sea and an end to the armoured counter-attack against the landings.

The appearance of German armour in front of 185th Brigade caused some concern in 3rd Division's HQ. The counter-attack and the ability of the enemy to reach the sea made the lodgement look increasingly vulnerable. It was evident that an advance on Caen was out of the question that day, and Gen Rennie decided that he needed to regroup before a new attack could be made. All units were told to dig in for the night and be prepared for enemy counter-attacks.

HOLDING AND EXPANDING THE BRIDGEHEAD

A group of German troops rest the side of the road. The surpr gained by the invasion and the rapid disintegration of German resistance on the beach often resulted in pockets of the ene retreating inland with no clear orders about where or how to regroup. (Bundesarchiv, 720/324/28A)

The initial reaction by the Allies to the events of D-Day was one of great satisfaction. There had not been the blood bath that so many pundits had envisaged and the British airborne landings had been completely successful, with Gen Gale's troops having seized all their objectives. The American airborne operations had been more scattered than the British, but they had not suffered the 50 per cent casualties that had been predicted in some quarters. American seaborne landings on Utah and Omaha had secured a foothold in Normandy and whilst those on Omaha were precarious, they were at least ashore. The British and Canadian landings over the beaches of Gold and Juno had allowed troops to get well inland and they were in little danger of being repulsed. In addition, the British 3rd Division's operations through Sword Beach had advanced over six miles towards Caen. Certainly, this first day of the invasion could be seen as a great success. A sound foothold had been gained and reinforcements were due to arrive over the next few days at a rate that would match anything the enemy could bring forward over roads harassed by Allied fighter-bombers. But there had been one major failure that day, one which would come back to haunt Montgomery over the next six weeks. His troops had failed to capture Caen.

The city of Caen was one of Montgomery's key objectives for 6 June. With Caen and its road network in Allied hands, the British would be able to advance from the beachhead into the good tank country around Falaise and the Germans would find it more difficult to counter-attack

the lodgement. Caen would also act as a cornerstone to the Allied defences, allowing the build-up of strength prior to a break-out into northern France. However, the 3rd Division's 185th and 9th Brigades did not make it to Caen on the first day of the invasion, and the enemy was determined that they never would. It was probably unreasonable to expect that such a small force, supported by just two tank battalions, could advance and hold such a large objective, especially against local troops and a powerful German armoured unit in the shape of 21st Panzer Division. The element of surprise had now been lost, and the British move towards Caen was an objective that was clear to the enemy. General der Artillerie Erich Marcks was adamant that his LXXXIV Corps, supported by Panzer forces, would never again allow the enemy to gain the initiative by surprise.

The main concern facing Montgomery on 7 June was whether his armies could achieve their build-up before the German Panzer divisions met them head on in a full counter-attack against the beachhead. The Allies had superiority in the air and the battlefield was well within the range of the big guns of the warships, but Monty needed infantry ashore to help absorb the armoured blow that was bound to fall. The two closest reserve Panzer units were 12th SS Panzer Division and Panzer Lehr Division, both fully equipped and of the highest calibre. Montgomery knew that these two divisions would soon be thrown against his beachhead and the prospect was quite alarming, but indecision in the German High Command would soon ease some of his immediate worries.

When news of the landings reached GFM Rommel in Germany, he started back for Normandy at once, reaching his headquarters that night. He immediately ordered that the American landings be sealed off by infantry and that a concerted armoured counter-attack be made from Caen against the British. The task of counter-attacking was assigned to the newly formed 1st SS Panzer Corps which, when complete, would contain 21st Panzer, 12th SS Panzer and Panzer Lehr Divisions. The corps, which was to be commanded by Obergruppenführer Sepp Dietrich, was ordered to start the attack immediately on 7 June, with Feuchtinger's 21st Panzers and those elements of the 12th SS Division that had reached the area. There was no time to wait for the arrival of Panzer Lehr, who were not expected to congregate at Caen before 8 June.

The direction of the attack would be between the British and Canadian lodgements, aimed at linking up with the German strongpoint at Douvres and those elements of 716th Division that still held out in Luc sur Mer. Soon after midnight, Standartenführer Kurt Meyer met with GenLt Richter and GenMaj Feuchtinger in a bunker near La Folie to plan the attack. Meyer, commander of the 25th SS Panzergrenadier Regiment of the 12th SS Panzer Division, was dismayed to hear that the

716th Division had been virtually wiped out and that Feuchtinger had only about 70 serviceable tanks left in his division after his abortive attack the previous day. Meyer, however, was confident that his troops, the pick of the Hitler Youth, could smash the British landings, predicting that he would throw the 'little fish' back into the sea.

21ST AND 12TH SS PANZER COUNTER-ATTACK

The 12th SS Panzer Division 'Hitlerjugend' was untried in battle, but was composed of fanatical young men from the Hitler Youth, led and strengthened by experienced officers and NCOs, many of whom came from the veteran 'Leibstandarte Adolf Hitler' division.

Meyer's regiment, which contained three infantry battalions, was the only one that had arrived in the area, but he was reinforced with the division's II Panzer Battalion and III Artillery Battalion. This *Kampfgruppe* (battlegroup) had about 90 PzKpfw IV at its disposal which, together with those of the 21st Panzers, would pitch around 160 tanks against the British and Canadians. (In the event, however, not all of the Mark IV tanks of the 12th SS arrived in time and only 50 were in place by 1400hrs on 7 June.)

The plan of attack was for the 21st Panzers to once again advance towards Lion sur Mer, whilst Meyer's SS troops attacked north-west from the area of Carpiquet airfield through the gap between the British and Canadians. The attacks, however, failed to progress as planned. Both divisions had to react to the actions of the British 3rd and Canadian 3rd Divisions. With daybreak Allied fighter-bombers began to harass the movement of Kampfgruppe Meyer, slowing down its concentration. Before Meyer could deploy his units for the joint attack, Feuchtinger's division once again found itself trying to stem the advance of the British 3rd Division through Lebisey Wood. Major-General Rennie had resumed his move on Caen that morning and was committing both his 185th and 9th Brigades against the city. The 185th Brigade's attack on Lebisey, led by 2nd Warwicks, was halted almost immediately, but amid heavy fighting. The Panzergrenadiers had spent the night reinforcing the area, preparing for their own attack and were well sited to repulse the British move. The 185th Brigade later tried again, with 1st Norfolks joining in the assault, but it was once more unable to gain entry into Lebisey itself.

Over on the 3rd Division's right, 9th Brigade began its advance on Caen with a move by 1st Royal Ulster Rifles and 1st King's Own Scottish Borderers along the axis, Periers-Mathieu-Le Mesnil towards Cambes. These infantry battalions had to fight their way through more units of Feuchtinger's division. Again the British were stopped by well-entrenched Panzergrenadiers, and by mid-afternoon the advance had stalled. The attacks had brought some success, for they had forced 21st Panzer Division to commit itself in a defensive role. The division was no longer able to disengage and regroup for its own counter-attack in support of Kampfgruppe Meyer.

Similar events were taking place over on the German's left flank. Canadian 3rd Division was advancing straight towards Meyer's assembly area with the result that he too became committed to action before he was ready to attack. The 'Hitlerjugend' troops fought exceptionally well, halting the Canadians in a bloody battle around Authie. Meyer's

German Panzergrenadier from 12th SS Panzer Division 'Hitlerjugend'. This young member of the Hitler Youth division is a leader of a machine gun squad and carries an MG42 slung about his neck. The average age of the soldiers in the division in 1943 was just 17. (Bundesarchiv 83/109/14A)

Driver R.P. Turnham hangs out his washing behind one of the concrete casemates of the 'Morris' strongpoint near Colleville. The German battery was captured just after midday on D-Day by 1st Suffolks. (Imperial War Museum, B5876)

This German convoy has been attacked by fighter-bombers. The smoke billowing from the burning trucks will act as a beacon to more Allied aircraft. In the rear of the Volkswagen 'Kubelwagen' one of its passengers scans the sky nervously, trying to stay one step ahead of the deadly 'jabos'. (Bundesarchiv, 301/1960/24)

battlegroup had stopped the Allied advance and prevented the capture of the strategically important Carpiquet airfield, but it had to commit the whole of its strength to do so, leaving nothing left with which to stage its own planned counter-attack against the beachhead.

On the eastern side of the British lodgement, MajGen Gale's paratroopers had also been in action that day. The arrival of 6th Airlanding and 1st Special Forces Brigades late the previous day had strengthened Gale's hold on the left flank of the landings. He was able to deploy these brigades in the north and south of his lodgement and give himself the satisfaction of holding a good all-round defensive position. His task was to defend his ground against enemy attempts to break through towards the Allied beachhead, and this is exactly what he did. Apart from some localised attacks to consolidate its position, British 6th Airborne Division assumed a defensive role. General Gale first 'tidied up' his sector by sending Brig Lovat's commandos to clear the enemy out of Franceville Plage in the north, and he used Brig Kindersley's airlanding brigade to push back the enemy in the south. This done, 6th Airborne Division's paras and Lovat's commandos set about tightening their grip on the area to the east of the Orne; a task that remained theirs until the great break-out from Normandy in August.

By the end of the second day, Sword Beach looked secure. British 3rd Division was close to Caen, with the front line pushed forward almost eight miles from the coast. Its left flank was secured by 6th Airborne, its right by the Canadians. In the skies over Normandy, Allied air forces had total command of the air. To its rear, the warships of the Royal Navy secured the sea lanes and dominated inland areas with their massive guns. Supplies and follow-up divisions were coming ashore to bolster the lodgement. It was now time for Montgomery to exploit the landings and push inland, always prepared for the inevitable confrontation with Rommel's gathering forces.

AFTERMATH

On 8 June attempts to capture Caen were renewed. Both the Canadians and British resumed their fight with 12th SS and 21st Panzer Divisions, the former having by then concentrated the whole of its force in the area around the city. The 12th SS launched counter-attacks against the Allied advance with a fanaticism and severity that was to be their hallmark in Normandy. It soon became clear to Montgomery that the enemy had also realised the significance of Caen and was determined to hold it at all costs. The city now became the main focus of Montgomery's strategy, and what had originally been just a divisional objective now became the goal of 2nd British Army.

On 10 June Montgomery made his first concentrated attack against Caen. With the German armoured divisions planted squarely to the north of the city he knew it could not be taken by frontal assault, so he decided to attack round each side using fresh troops who had arrived by sea. The 51st Highland Division and 4th Armoured Brigade were to attack from the airborne lodgement to the east of Caen, whilst the 7th Armoured Division made a wide sweeping move through Villers Bocage to get behind the newly arrived Panzer Lehr Division. Coincidentally, Rommel and von Rundstedt also planned a counter-attack in exactly the opposite direction at about the same time. Panzer Lehr was to move against British 7th Armoured Division while 21st Panzer Division once again attacked the airborne lodgement on the Allied left flank.

This knocked-out concrete gun emplacement has been taken over by the Royal Navy. With the beaches still under occasional shell fire and with the Luftwaffe putting in a few bombing runs, a naval beach group has found it prudent to have some cover over its head. (Imperial War Museum, B6381)

Lieutenant-Colonel Peter Young, CO of 6 Commando, gives instructions to two of his camouflaged snipers who are going to keep watch on a house on the edge of Breville that overlooks the lines of the 6th Airborne Division. (Imperial War Museum, B5761)

Both attacks failed. The 21st Panzer's effort ran straight into the gathering 51st Division and was stopped dead, but in doing so blunted the organised drive by the Highlanders. British 7th Armoured Division had its advance turned at Villers Bocage when 25 tanks, 14 half-tracks and 14 carriers were knocked out in the town in one short action. Panzer Lehr then became embroiled with the British armour and was unable to mount its own counter-attack.

Montgomery tried again to take Caen with a major offensive called Operation Epsom, which was carried out by British VIII Corps, commanded by Lieutenant-General O'Connor. Its aim was to advance

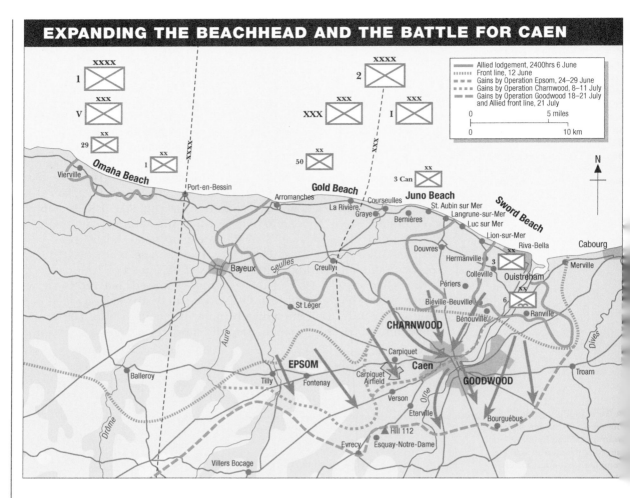

towards Caen drawing the enemy Panzer divisions on to it whilst the Americans made progress in the west, aiming for a much wider encirclement of the German forces defending the city and pressing for a break-out of Normandy into northern France. Monty felt that it was imperative to apply continual pressure to the German armoured divisions, keeping them off balance and unable to regroup for a combined counter-offensive, whilst at the same time attempting to gain control of Caen.

Operation Epsom was not a complete success. The 15th Scottish Division made some gains, albeit after suffering great casualties, and managed to take a bridgehead over the River Odon. The 43rd Wessex Division and 11th Armoured Division consolidated these gains and pushed on to Hill 112, allowing the front line to be extended, but no break-through onto the open ground to the south of Caen materialised. Once again, however, the timing of the British advance interfered with a counter-attack being organised by the enemy. Montgomery's troops had attacked at a critical moment for Rommel, striking as he was moving the 2nd, 9th and 10th SS Panzer Divisions into the area for a major thrust by II SS Corps towards the sea. The result was that each side pounded the other to a halt, with Caen still remaining firmly in German hands.

Next came Operation Charnwood, the frontal attack on Caen carried out by British I Corps. It was a spectacular affair, preceded by a massive air

days after the landings,
bers of a tank crew from
Squadron of the 13th/18th
sars sit beside their Sherman
write letters home or just
the opportunity to catch up
ome sleep. The squadron
been in action with the
orne division near the
ouville bridges, helping to
with counter-attacks by
th Panzergrenadier Regiment.
erial War Museum, B5425)

German motorcycle
mbination passes a sign
rning of low-flying Allied
craft. It was a threat that
nained constant throughout
whole of the war in
rth-West Europe.
ndesarchiv 585/2208/3)

raid by the RAF when 450 heavy bombers attempted to eliminate the German strongpoints in front of the city. The raid proved to be a futile effort as most enemy positions survived, but the ancient city was reduced to a pile of smoking rubble. The next day, 8 July, British 3rd and 59th Divisions together with Canadian 3rd Division attacked the city. After two days of bitter fighting they reached the centre of Caen but could not get across the River Orne to the southern outskirts of the city. More than a month after D-Day, Montgomery was still not the complete master of Caen.

German prisoners wait patiently on board a beached LCT for the craft to be floated by the incoming tide. They will be taken to prisoner of war camps in Britain. (Imperial War Museum, B5135)

The final capture of the city was achieved during Operation 'Goodwood'. The operation saw an armoured thrust from out of the airborne lodgement on the left side of the Allied line with a view to encircling the city and breaking out into open tank country toward Falaise. The 7th, 11th and Guards Armoured Divisions, together with British 3rd Infantry Division, launched their attack on 18 July sweeping southwards around the eastern side of Caen. At the same time, 2nd Canadian Division attacked round the western side of the city and 3rd Canadian Division pushed through the centre. At first, progress was good and the capture of the whole of Caen was completed, but the massive offensive failed in its task to break through the German line. The enemy was pushed back, but held the Allied advance along the Bourguebus Ridge. line of 88mm anti-tank guns brought the armoured attack to a halt and the operation petered out with great material loss.

Montgomery's war of attrition against German armoured units around Caen did, however, enable the Americans to make progress in the west. Montgomery had attracted the bulk of German Panzer divisions onto the British side of the lodgement as they continued to defend the cornerstone on which German strategy in Normandy depended. They knew that a break-through at Caen would open up a direct route into the French interior and enable the Allies to encircle German Seventh Army. Ultimately, this was what happened, although the break-out and encirclement was initiated from the American side of the lodgement when Gen Bradley's 1st Army broke out of the confines of the Normandy *bocage* and Gen Patton's 3rd army swung south and east to get behind the German forces and open the road to Paris. By the middle of August the German collapse in Normandy was complete and its Seventh Army had been annihilated.

THE BATTLEFIELD TODAY

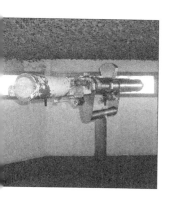

Sword Beach and the area of British 6th Airborne's operations east of the River Orne lie in a part of Normandy now popular with holidaymakers. In the summer the area swarms with visitors, most of whom are intent on enjoying the delights that a seaside resort can bring, particularly the magnificent wide sandy beaches that are so common in this part of France. But visitors to Normandy seeking evidence of the area's recent violent history will, likewise, not be disappointed.

There are many memorials dotted throughout the area in recognition of the sacrifice made by the men involved in the D-Day landings. Also to be seen are various weapons and vehicles that serve to illustrate the types that were present during the action. Much of this equipment is not original to the battle, but was brought to the area later. There are, however, some veteran pieces of equipment that actually took part in the assault, though these are rare.

At Bénouville the original lifting-bridge across the Orne Canal has been removed to make way for a larger modern structure, but the new bridge's similar shape gives the visitor a good impression of the site as it was in 1944. Still there alongside the bridge, dispensing refreshment to the traveller, is the Café Gondrée, once used as a dressing station during the battle and the first house in France to be liberated. Opposite the café is a real veteran of the landings in the shape of a Centaur tank. It came ashore with 5th (Independent) Battery of the Royal Marine Armoured Support Group at La Brèche on Sword Beach, but was knocked out shortly after landing. On the eastern side of the bridge,

there is a gunpit housing the 50mm anti-tank weapon that was present during Maj Howard's raid. It has been renovated and re-sited, but remains largely as it was when captured. A few hundred yards to the east is the Airborne Museum, which houses relics of the landings. In its grounds is the original Pegasus Bridge over which 'D' Company of the 2nd Oxs and Bucks stormed during the first minutes of 6 June.

Most impressive of the airborne locations is the Merville battery. Its four casemates, set in quiet green fields, now form part of an excellent museum complex. Number One casemate was renovated by Royal Engineers in 1982 and now houses a display of artefacts associated with its capture. Within the battery grounds the German command bunker and personnel shelters can also be seen.

On Sword Beach, along the seafront at La Brèche, many of the seaside villas that were present in 1944 have been rebuilt and can often be identified from wartime photographs. Nowadays these villas, which are no longer isolated from each other by large gardens, merge with modern holiday homes and housing estates to form a continuous ribbon of development all the way along the beach eastwards to Ouistreham/Riva Bella. The rear of the flat beach is still edged by sand dunes, held together by grassy knolls, behind which the assault waves of British 3rd Division sheltered from enemy fire. Strongpoint 'Cod' has been buried by houses, but its site can be traced by a network of quiet roads that mark the perimeter of the fortified area. The point where Lovat's 1st Special Service Brigade came ashore is celebrated by a memorial located opposite a concrete casemate that once housed a 75mm gun.

At Riva Bella the Casino area captured by Captain Kieffer and his French commandos has been built over. The modern Casino sits squarely on the site of the old. There are a few tangible remains of the German strongpoint, such as the anti-tank 'dragon's teeth' that run between beach huts to the rear of the site, and a casemate topped by an

The memorial that marks the site of the landings made by Lord Lovat's commandos on D-Day. Opposite the monument is the concrete emplacement that housed a 75mm gun sited to fire along the length of Sword Beach. (Ken Ford)

armoured cupola that forms the base of the monument to the commandos. A good depiction of the capture of the strongpoint can be found in the Commando Museum opposite the present Casino.

Further along the seafront is the site of the six-gun battery at Ouistreham, which was captured by 4 Commando. This was an open construction defended by machine gun posts and wire. Although little of the physical structures remain, the sites of the guns can still be traced. Just behind this area is one of the best examples of a modern museum being housed in a contemporary building, in this case a building that actually played its part in the D-Day battles. Standing 55ft (17m) high amongst suburban streets and gardens, with only a large observation slit visible to the outside, is the German fire control post for the defences of the River Orne estuary. The building's equipment supplied range and direction information to the surrounding artillery batteries. On 6 June the post received a lucky direct hit from the cruiser HMS *Frobisher*, which put it out of action. The troops inside still remained active, however, and even interfered with the attack made on the Ouistreham battery by 4 Commando. At the time, Lovat's men were occupied on other tasks and did not attempt to capture the structure. It was not until 9 June that its garrison surrendered to a Royal Engineer officer and three men. Lieutenant Bob Orell and his team blew in the armoured door and invited the Germans to come out. Fifty artillerymen gave themselves up. Today the post houses a museum devoted to Hitler's Atlantic Wall. It contains excellent exhibitions on each of its levels. On the top floor, looking out through the narrow observation slit, is a working German optical rangefinder, from which one can gain an excellent view of Sword Beach.

Of the land battles fought to extend the lodgement, virtually all of the German field works that defended inland positions have been erased, but there is still much to be seen of the fortified complex 'Hillman' lying just to the south-west of Colleville Montgomery. The strongpoint was captured by 1st Suffolks on D-Day, and there is a

ABOVE **The grave of Lt Den Brotheridge, 'D' Company 2nd Oxs and Bucks Light Infantry, the first British soldie to die during the invasion. He rests amongst his comrades close to the wall of Ranville churchyard alongside a dedication from the Gondrée family. (Ken Ford)**

ABOVE, LEFT **The Commonwea War Graves Commission's cemetery close by the church a Ranville. More paratroopers are buried just inside the wall of the churchyard. (Ken Ford)**

memorial to the battalion on a concrete bunker close to the road. Behind this, spread throughout a series of grassy meadows, are the visible remains of many other defensive structures and steel cupolas that fortified the site. It should be remembered that, like an iceberg, what you see on the surface is only a small part of the huge network of bunkers and passages that lie underground.

Perhaps the most pertinent of the memorials that remind us of the great sacrifices made during D-Day are the cemeteries that mark the area. In the Commonwealth War Graves Cemetery at Ranville, MajGen Gale's fallen paratroopers lie side by side with the dead of the later battles for Caen and many of their German opponents. Alongside, in the walled enclosure of Ranville Church, are the graves of more of 6th Airborne's heroes, including that of Lt Den Brotheridge, the first British soldier to be killed in the invasion. Many of the dead who fell during the Normandy battles can be found in the other British cemeteries at Douvres La Déliverande, Cambes en Plaine and Hermanville. Please pay them a visit and honour the sacrifice made by the heroes of Operation Overlord.

ORDER OF BATTLE

Allied Forces, Sword Beach Assault Phase, 6 June 1944

Allied Supreme Commander – **Gen Dwight D. Eisenhower**

British 21st Army Group – **Gen Sir Bernard L. Montgomery**

British Second Army – **LtGen Sir Miles Dempsey**

British I Corps – **LtGen John Crocker**

British 6th Airborne Division – **MajGen Richard N. Gale**
- 3rd Parachute Brigade – **Brig James Hill**
  - 8th Parachute Battalion – LtCol Alistair Pearson
  - 9th Parachute Battalion – LtCol Terence Otway
  - 1st Canadian Parachute Battalion – LtCol George Bradbrook
- 5th Parachute Brigade – **Brig Nigel Poett**
  - 7th Parachute Battalion – LtCol Pine Coffin
  - 12th Parachute Battalion – LtCol Johnny Johnson
  - 13th Parachute Battalion – LtCol Luard
- 6th Airlanding Brigade – **Brig Hugh Kindersley**
  - A Coy., 12th Battalion, The Devonshire Regiment
  - 2nd Battalion, The Oxfordshire & Buckinghamshire Light Infantry
  - 1st Battalion, The Royal Ulster Rifles

British 3rd Infantry Division – **MajGen Tom Rennie**
- 8th Infantry Brigade – **Brig E. Cass**
  - 1st Battalion, The Suffolk Regiment
  - 2nd Battalion, The East Yorkshire Regiment
  - 1st Battalion, The South Lancashire Regiment
- 9th Infantry Brigade – **Brig J. C. Cunningham**
  - 2nd Battalion, The Lincolnshire Regiment
  - 1st Battalion, The King's Own Scottish Borderers
  - 2nd Battalion, The Royal Ulster Rifles
- 185th Infantry Brigade – **Brig K. P. Smith**
  - 2nd Battalion, The Royal Warwickshire Fusiliers
  - 1st Battalion, The Royal Norfolk Regiment
  - 2nd Battalion, The King's Shropshire Light Infantry

  7th Field Regiment, Royal Artillery
  33rd Field Regiment, Royal Artillery
  76th Field Regimen,t Royal Artillery
  20th Anti-tank Regiment, Royal Artillery
  92nd Light Anti-aircraft Regiment, Royal Artillery
  53rd Medium Regiment, Royal Artillery (attached for landings)

  2nd Battalion, The Middlesex Regiment (machine gun)

  3rd Reconnaissance Regiment, Royal Armoured Corps

  101st Beach Sub-Area
  - 5th King's Regiment (Beach Group)
  - 1st Oxfordshire & Buckinghamshire Light Infantry (Beach Group)

1st Special Service Brigade – **Brig Lord Lovat**
- 3 Commando
- 4 Commando
- 6 Commando
- 45 (Royal Marine) Commando

4th Special Service Brigade – **Brig B.W. Leicester**
- 41 (Royal Marine) Commando

27th Armoured Brigade – **Brig G.E. Prior Palmer**
- 13th/18th Royal Hussars
- 1st East Riding Yeomanry
- The Staffordshire Yeomanry

th Armoured Division – **MajGen Sir Percy C.S. Hobart**
- 30th Armoured Brigade – **Brig N.W. Duncan**
  - 22nd Dragoons
  - 2nd County of London Yeomanry (Westminster Dragoons)
  - 141st Regiment, Royal Armoured Corps
- 1st Assault Brigade, Royal Engineers – **Brig G.L. Watkinson**
  - 5th Assault Regiment, Royal Engineers

German Forces

German Supreme Commander - **Adolf Hitler**

German Commander-in-Chief (West) - **GFM Gerd von Rundstedt**

German Army Group B - **GFM Erwin Rommel**

German Seventh Army - **GenObst Friedrich Dollmann**

German LXXXIV Corps - **General der Artillerie Erich Marcks**

German 716th Infantry Division - **GenLt Wilhelm Richter**
- 726th Infantry Regiment
  - I Battalion
  - II Battalion
  - III Battalion
  - 441st East Battalion
- 736th Infantry Regiment - **Obst Krug**
  - I Battalion
  - II Battalion
  - III Battalion
  - 642nd East Battalion
- 1716th Artillery Regiment
  - I/1716 Artillery Battalion
  - II/1716 Artillery Battalion

  716th Reconnaissance Company

  716th Engineer Battalion

German 21st Panzer Division - **GenMaj Edgar Feuchtinger**
- 100th Panzer Regiment - **Obst von Oppeln-Bronikowski**
  - I Battalion
  - II Battalion
- 125th Panzergrenadier Regiment
  - I Battalion
  - II Battalion
- 192nd Panzergrenadier Regiment - **Obstlt Rauch**
  - I Battalion
  - II Battalion

  200th Panzer Reconnaissance Battalion

  200th Sturmgeschütz Battalion

  200th Panzerjäger Battalion

  155th Panzer Artillery Regiment
  - I Battalion
  - II Battalion
  - III Battalion

  305th Army Flak Battalion

  220th Panzer Pioneer Battalion

BIBLIOGRAPHY

Ambrose, Stephen E., *Pegasus Bridge*, Allen and Unwin (London, 1984)

Anon, *Airborne Forces*, Air Ministry (London, 1951)

Anon, *Operation 'Neptune' Landings in Normandy, June 1944*, HMSO (London, 1994)

Carell, Paul, *Invasion - They're Coming!* , George Harrap (London, 1962)

Crookenden, Napier, *Dropzone Normandy*, Ian Allen (London, 1976)

Ellis, Maj L. F., *Victory In The West*, HMSO (London, 1962)

Gale, LtGen Richard, *With The Sixth Airborne Division in Normandy*, Sampson, Low, Marston & Co (London, 1948)

Golley, John, *The Big Drop*, Janes (London, 1982)

Harclerode, Peter, *'Go To It!'*, Caxton Editions (London, 2000)

Hastings, Max, *Overlord*, Michael Joseph (London, 1984)

McDougall, Murdoch C., *Swiftly They Struck*, Odhams (London, 1954)

McNish, Robin, *Iron Division*, Ian Allen (London, 1978)

Meyer, Hubert, *The History of the 12th SS Panzer Division 'Hitlerjugend'*, J. J. Fedorowicz (Winnipeg, Canada, 1994)

Mitcham, Samuel W., *Hitler's Legions*, Leo Cooper (London, 1985)

Morgan, LtGen Sir Frederick, *Overture To Overlord*, Hodder & Stoughton (London, 1950)

Ramsey, Winston G. (ed), *D Day Then and Now*, Battle of Britain Prints International (London, 1995)

Saunders, Hilary St George, *The Green Beret*, Michael Joseph (London, 1949)

Scarfe, Norman, *Assault Division*, Collins (London, 1947)

Wilmot, Chester, *The Struggle For Europe*, Collins (London, 1952)

NDEX